O9-BHJ-860

34
73
36
1995

ORIOLE

R0171897405

Jane Austen's Pride and prejudice.

DATE DUE    8/00

| | | | |
|---|---|---|---|
| NOV 18 2000 | | | |
| FEB 28 2001 | | | |
| APR 23 2001 | | | |
| MAY 21 2001 | | | |
| AUG 27 2001 | | | |
| | | | |
| | | | |
| | | | |
| | | | |
| | | | |
| | | | |
| | | | |
| | | | |
| | | | |
| | | | |
| | | | |
| | | | |

DEMCO 38-296

Jane Austen's
# PRIDE AND PREJUDICE

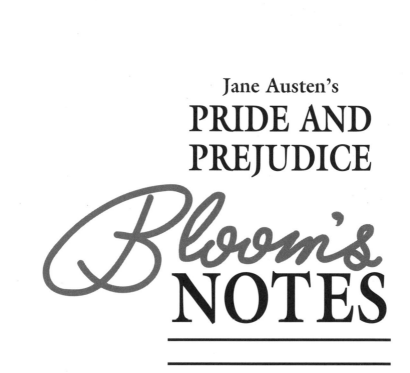

# *Bloom's* NOTES

A CONTEMPORARY
LITERARY VIEWS BOOK

Edited and with an Introduction by
# HAROLD BLOOM

CHICAGO PUBLIC LIBRARY
ORIOLE PARK BRANCH
5201 N. OKETO      60656

© 1996 by Chelsea House Publishers, a division of Main Line Book Co.

Introduction © 1996 by Harold Bloom

All rights reserved. No part of this publication may be reproduced or transmitted in any form or by any means without the written permission of the publisher.

Printed and bound in the United States of America.

3 5 7 9 8 6 4 2

*Cover illustration:* Photofest

Library of Congress Cataloging-in-Publication Data

Jane Austen's Pride and prejudice / Harold Bloom, editor.
p.   cm. — (Bloom's Notes)
"Books by Jane Austen":
Includes bibliographical references and index.
Summary: Includes a brief biography of the author, thematic and structural analysis of the work, critical views, and an index of themes and ideas.
ISBN 0-7910-3669-3
1. Austen, Jane, 1775–1817. Pride and prejudice. 2. Young women in literature. 3. Courtship in literature. [1. Austen, Jane, 1775–1817. Pride and prejudice. 2. English literature—History and criticism.] I. Bloom, Harold. II. Series.
PR4034.P73J36 1995
823'.7—dc20
95-34518
CIP
AC

Chelsea House Publishers
1974 Sproul Road, Suite 400
P.O. Box 914
Broomall, PA 19008-0914

R0171897405

CHICAGO PUBLIC LIBRARY
ORIOLE PARK BRANCH
5201 N. OKETO        60656

# Contents

# User's Guide

This volume is designed to present biographical, critical, and bibliographical information on Jane Austen and *Pride and Prejudice.* Following Harold Bloom's introduction, there appears a detailed biography of the author, discussing the major events in her life and her important literary works. Then follows a thematic and structural analysis of the work, in which significant themes, patterns, and motifs are traced. An annotated list of characters supplies brief information on the chief characters in the work.

A selection of critical extracts, derived from previously published material by leading critics, then follows. The extracts consist of statements by the author on her work, early reviews of the work, and later evaluations down to the present day. The items are arranged chronologically by date of first publication. A bibliography of Austen's writings (including a complete listing of all books she wrote, cowrote, edited, and translated, and selected posthumous publications), a list of additional books and articles on her and on *Pride and Prejudice,* and an index of themes and ideas conclude the volume.

---

**Harold Bloom** is Sterling Professor of the Humanities at Yale University and Henry W. and Albert A. Berg Professor of English at the New York University Graduate School. He is the author of twenty books and the editor of more than thirty anthologies of literature and literary criticism.

Professor Bloom's works include *Shelley's Mythmaking* (1959), *The Visionary Company* (1961), *Blake's Apocalypse* (1963), *Yeats* (1970), *A Map of Misreading* (1975), *Kabbalah and Criticism* (1975), and *Agon: Towards a Theory of Revisionism* (1982). *The Anxiety of Influence* (1973) sets forth Professor Bloom's provocative theory of the literary relationships between the great writers and their predecessors. His most recent books are *The American Religion* (1992) and *The Western Canon* (1994).

Professor Bloom earned his Ph.D. from Yale University in 1955 and has served on the Yale faculty since then. He is a 1985 MacArthur Foundation Award recipient and served as the Charles Eliot Norton Professor of Poetry at Harvard University in 1987–88. He is currently the editor of the Chelsea House series Major Literary Characters and Modern Critical Views, and other Chelsea House series in literary criticism.

# Introduction

## HAROLD BLOOM

If the authentic test for a great novel is rereading, and the joys of yet further rereadings, then *Pride and Prejudice* can rival any novel ever written. Though Jane Austen, unlike Shakespeare, practices an art of rigorous exclusion, she seems to me finally the most Shakespearean novelist in the language. When Shakespeare wishes to, he can make all his personages, major and minor, speak in voices entirely their own, self-consistent and utterly different from one another. Austen, with the similar illusion of ease, does the same. Since voice in both writers is an image of personality and also of character, the reader of Austen encounters an astonishing variety of selves in her socially confined world. Though that world is essentially a secularized culture, the moral vision dominating it remains that of the Protestant sensibility. Austen's heroines waver in one judgment or another, but they hold fast to the right of private judgment as the self's fortress. What they call "affection" we term "love," of the enduring rather than the Romantic variety, and when they judge a man to be "amiable," it is akin to whatever superlative each of us may favor for an admirable, human person. Where they may differ from us, but more in degree than in kind, is in their profound reliance upon the soul's exchanges of mutual esteem with other souls. In *Pride and Prejudice* and *Emma* in particular, your accuracy in estimating the nature and value of another soul is intimately allied to the legitimacy of your self-esteem, your valid pride.

The moral comedy of the misunderstandings between Elizabeth Bennet and Darcy has been compared, by several critics, to the combat of wit between Beatrice and Benedick in Shakespeare's *Much Ado About Nothing*. As a comparison, this has limited usefulness: Elizabeth is not primarily a wit or a social ironist. Her true Shakespearean precursor is Rosalind in *As You Like It*. Rosalind resorts to furious wit in properly squelching Jacques and Touchstone, but her fundamental strength is a sure sense of self, with the wisdom that only an accurate self-estimate can bring. Such wisdom transcends detachment and welcomes a generous concern with other selves. It leads to a pride that is also playful, which is an intense contrast to Darcy's implacable pride. His sense of self relies upon an immense conviction of personal as well as societal eminence. We cannot dispute his conviction; he is intellectually formidable, morally fair-minded, and a better judge of character than Elizabeth sometimes proves to be. But his aggressiveness is excessive, despite Elizabeth's final, justified verdict: "He is frequently amiable." There is a touch of the quixotic in Elizabeth, while Darcy stands outside what could be termed the order of play. Tact without playfulness can yield too readily to moral zeal; but the quixotic not only can be tactless, it can decay into misguided exuberance.

Such reflections, though germane to *Pride and Prejudice,* are sadly abstract when applied to the lively comedy of the novel. Surprise keeps breaking in, and nothing turns out as anyone in the book expects. We are indeed in a Shakespearean world, as random in its way as Rosalind's Forest of Arden. Only the level firmness of Austen's narrative voice holds together a social world that borders oddly upon the bizarre, for everyone in it is rather more idiosyncratic than at first they appear to be. *Pride and Prejudice* has an authentic monster in Mr. Collins, a poseur in Wickham, a tyrant of pride in Lady Catherine, and a master of destructive satire in Mr. Bennet. There is a marvelous comic tension between Austen's seemingly normative tone and the eccentric personages who perpetually render the story more vivid and more strange.

Irony, which essentially is saying one thing while meaning another, is Austen's characteristic mode. Austen's irony, while endlessly genial, unsettles all her meanings. Where we seem most assured of the happiness or perfection attained by her heroines, we learn to look more closely and to surmise the implied reservations of this ironic vision. A great master of metaphor, Austen is also a genius of the unsaid: she expects the astute reader to say it for her. Not that Austen, in the manner of her Darcy, is a triumph of tact; she is more in the mode of her Elizabeth Bennet, and is a triumph of playfulness. In some ways, Austen is more like Shakespeare's Rosalind than Elizabeth ever could be, and so Austen's largest triumph is in the sheer psychic and spiritual health of her magnificent wit and invention. ❖

# Biography of Jane Austen

Jane Austen was born at Steventon in Hampshire, England, on December 16, 1775, the seventh of eight children of the Reverend George Austen and Cassandra Leigh Austen. She was educated at home by her father, then in 1783 she was sent with her sister Cassandra to attend a school run by a Mrs. Cawley (first at Oxford, then at Southampton), where she almost died of putrid fever. During 1784–85 Jane and Cassandra went to the Abbey School in Reading.

Austen started writing around 1787, perhaps inspired by the plays put on by her family in the neighboring barn or in the parsonage where her father was rector. Among her juvenilia are *Love and Freindship* (so spelled on the manuscript), written around 1790 and being a burlesque of love stories and romances; *History of England* (1791), as by "a partial, prejudiced, and ignorant historian"; *Catharine,* an unfinished novel about an orphan girl; and several other works. She included many of these writings in a three-volume manuscript collection entitled, respectively, *Volume the First, Volume the Second,* and *Volume the Third,* which she completed copying by 1793.

During 1794–96 Austen wrote a novel entitled *Elinor and Marianne,* followed in 1796 by *First Impressions.* The latter was offered in 1797 to a publisher named Cadell but was rejected by him without a reading. In that year Austen began rewriting *Elinor and Marianne* under the title *Sense and Sensibility.* In 1798 she wrote a novel entitled *Susan;* this parody of the "Gothic" novel was sold to a publisher for £10 in 1803 but never appeared, and was published only posthumously in a revised version under the title *Northanger Abbey.* Around 1799 Austen wrote another novel entitled *Lady Susan,* while an unfinished novel entitled *The Watsons* probably dates from between 1800 and 1805.

In 1801 Austen's family moved to Bath. Around this time Jane apparently had a love affair with a clergyman. The next year she received a marriage proposal from Harris Bigg-Wither, a friend of one of her brothers, but she turned him down because she did not love him. Austen's nephew James Austen-Leigh has provided a vivid portrait of his aunt during this period:

> In person she was very attractive; her figure was rather tall and slender, her step light and firm, and her whole appearance expressive of health and animation. In complexion she was a clear brunette with a rich colour; she had full round cheeks, with mouth and nose well formed, light hazel eyes, and brown hair forming natural curls close round her face. If not so regularly handsome as her sister, yet her countenance had a peculiar charm of its own to the eyes of most beholders.

Regrettably, the only authentic portrait of Austen in existence is a sketch done by her sister Cassandra.

A year after her father's death in 1805, the family moved again to Southampton, and then, in 1809, to the village of Chawton, near Alton in Hampshire. Each move represented a downward step on the socioeconomic scale. During this time, however, Austen's writing finally began to see print. *Sense and Sensibility* was published in 1811, although only as "by a Lady." Austen then revised *First Impressions,* and it appeared as *Pride and Prejudice* in 1813. *Mansfield Park,* begun in 1811, was published in 1814, followed by *Emma* (1815). Some scholars believe that this novel is an extensive reworking of *The Watsons. Persuasion,* her last novel, was written in 1817. In May of that year the family went to Winchester to seek medical attention for Jane, who had developed Addison's disease. She died two months later, on July 18, 1817.

Much of Austen's work appeared posthumously, beginning with the joint publication of *Northanger Abbey* and *Persuasion* in 1818. In the 1920s her juvenilia began to appear, as well as a fragment of a novel, later known as *Sanditon,* written in early 1817. Much of this work was edited by R. W. Chapman, whose editions remain authoritative.

Over the years several writers have attempted to complete some of Austen's fragmentary works. In 1923 L. Oulton published a completion of *The Watsons,* followed five years later by another completion by Edith Brown (Austen's great-grandniece) and Frances Brown. Yet another completion of *The Watsons* was written by John Coates and published in 1958. *Sanditon* was completed by Anne Telscombe (1975), and Phyllis Anne Karr used Austen's fragment of *Lady Susan* as the basis of a novel. Sequels to several of Austen's completed novels have also been written. ✢

# Thematic and
# Structural Analysis

Jane Austen's *Pride and Prejudice* is a social comedy set in the provincial district of Hertfordshire, England, around the end of the eighteenth century. The plot, as the first sentence of the novel announces, is about marriage. Austen begins with the maxim that "a single man in possession of a good fortune must be in want of a wife." Marriage is a constant pursuit in Austen's comic world. Mothers exult over their daughters' conquests and administer poisoned sympathy at their neighbors' failures. Local balls and parties are a source of continuous gossip and speculation. Any marital news travels fast among the ingrown community.

The key stumbling block to marriage, as the title suggests, is a disparity in social class. Social distinctions can be subtle and are not equally apparent to all Austen's characters. Her wry class perceptions often emerge most sharply through the conversation of her characters. Much of the novel is conducted in dialogues that range in style from wittily combative to obtusely absurd.

The novel's heroine is Elizabeth Bennet, who comes from a respectable landed family but has had none of the amenities of an upper-class London upbringing. She and her older sister Jane are intelligent, well-bred young women, but her three younger sisters, encouraged by a flighty mother, are silly and flirtatious. As the Bennet daughters have only a tiny income and no brother to inherit the estate, their prospects for exceptional marriages seem slim. This does not deter their unflagging mother, whose greatest social triumph would be to find husbands for her girls.

The story begins when the opportunity for such a triumph arrives in the person of a wealthy single gentleman, Mr. Bingley, who rents the neighboring estate of Netherfield. "What a fine thing for our girls!" Mrs. Bennet exclaims. The first several chapters cover the social formalities observed in making his acquaintance—visits paid, calls returned, invitations extended—which culminate in a local ball of Hertfordshire. There, Mr. Bingley arrives with a party from London: two sisters, his brother-in-law, and his friend Mr. Darcy (**chapter three**). Bingley is immediately declared "good looking and gentlemanlike," while Darcy, who only dances with Bingley's sisters and remains aloof to the rest of the company, is soon dismissed as "a most disagreeable" man. Elizabeth feels slighted when she overhears Bingley trying to persuade Darcy to dance with her. He refuses, assessing her as only "tolerable."

The next morning the two eldest Bennet sisters discuss the ball. Jane admits that she admires Bingley, who has paid particular attention to her. Bingley and Darcy review the evening as well, but while Bingley is effusive in his praise, Darcy finds little to applaud. The excitement also necessitates visits around town, where Mrs. Bennet triumphs over Jane's success. Nonetheless, as their socializing together continues, Darcy finds himself increasingly taken with Elizabeth's wit and beauty. In **chapter six**, at a dinner party, a pompous Sir Lucas tries to persuade him to dance with Elizabeth, but while he is willing, she wryly refuses.

Mrs. Bennet's next social coup is Jane's invitation to dine at the Bingleys'. In **chapter seven**, oblivious to her daughter's welfare, she concocts a scheme to procure Jane a longer stay: She sends Jane to dinner on horseback with a rainstorm threatening. Jane gets drenched, catches a bad cold, and is forced to stay in bed for several days. The next morning Elizabeth visits her sister, walking three miles through the muddy fields. Her windswept, mud-spattered appearance shocks Miss Bingley, who ridicules Elizabeth behind her back but finds it impossible to get Darcy to join in her criticism. Meanwhile Elizabeth spends all day with Jane and gratefully accepts an invitation to stay until her sister recovers. This necessitates some socializing with Bingley's set. On joining the party that evening Elizabeth observes Miss Bingley's avid pursuit of Mr. Darcy. Miss Bingley meanwhile displays a double-edged graciousness to Elizabeth, praising Darcy's sister and lecturing her guest on the nature of a truly "accomplished woman"—everything Miss Bennet is not. Elizabeth is amused by this display of snobbery and counters playfully.

The next day Mrs. Bennet visits her daughter, showing little motherly concern but much eagerness to please Mr. Bingley. Elizabeth is embarrassed, and the Bingley sisters, once she leaves, mock her mother gleefully. That evening in the drawing room Miss Bingley dotes on an unresponsive Darcy, who finds himself increasingly taken with Elizabeth's irreverent, playful spirit. Miss Bingley grows jealous and begins to tease Darcy in private about his impending marriage to Miss Bennet, dwelling on the charming in-laws he will acquire.

Meanwhile, Jane begins to recover, and Elizabeth observes with delight Bingley's sincere concern for her comfort (**chapter eleven**). The drawing room drama continues, and that evening, drawn into playful banter with Darcy, Elizabeth accuses him of self-importance. He replies affectionately that Elizabeth's only defect is her tendency "wilfully to misunderstand" people. In this scene Austen set out the two poles of her title. Just as the aloof Mr. Darcy suffers from pride, Elizabeth, impulsively disliking him, errs in her prejudice.

The stay at Netherfield soon ends, much to Miss Bingley's relief and Mrs. Bennet's disappointment. The Bennets are soon caught up in another visit. Mr. Collins, Mr. Bennet's cousin and heir to the estate, has announced a visit. Mrs. Bennet first declares her aversion to this "odious man" who has had the audacity to be the next male kin, but when he arrives and intimates that he is seeking a wife, her opinion changes. Mr. Bennet soon concludes that his cousin is "as absurd as he had hoped" and leaves him to the female members. They suffer through his stilted compliments, pompous pronouncements, and effusive praise of his patroness, Lady Catherine de Bourgh.

Meanwhile, the local social scene is enlivened by the arrival of a militia company full of dashing young officers. On a walk into town, Elizabeth and her sisters, accompanied by Mr. Collins, meet the latest enlister, the handsome Mr. Wickham. As they are being introduced, Bingley and Darcy ride by and stop to greet the ladies. Elizabeth notices that Darcy and Wickham recognize each other but barely deign to greet.

In **chapter sixteen** Elizabeth meets Wickham again during a dinner party. She immediately likes his charming, open manner and is flattered when he confides to her his unhappy past with Darcy. He tells her that the late Mr. Darcy had been his godfather and patron and had bequeathed a living to him, but that the present Darcy, jealous and spiteful, had dishonorably ignored his father's will. Thus Wickham had been forced to join the army. Elizabeth is scandalized and urges Wickham to make his grievances public, but he insists on protecting the family name. Elizabeth confides her information to Jane, who refuses to think badly of Darcy. They let their secret rest while anticipating the next social adventure—a ball given by Bingley.

The ball, which takes place in **chapter eighteen**, proves a challenge to Elizabeth. She is first obliged to dance with Mr. Collins, whose attentions have become obvious. Then Mr. Darcy asks her to dance. Their conversation is awkward, exacerbated by Elizabeth's accusative allusions to Wickham. The evening continues badly. Her mother gleefully advertises Jane's expected engagement, her sister Mary embarrasses herself at the piano, her youngest sisters flirt wildly, and her cousin tediously introduces himself to Darcy, who he has learned is the nephew of Lady Catherine. Elizabeth is mortified.

The next day Mr. Collins declares himself to Elizabeth (**chapter nineteen**). Much to the horror of her mother, she refuses him. Mr. Collins feels stung and pompously revokes his offer but then continues to stay out his visit. During this awkward period Elizabeth gratefully welcomes her friend Charlotte Lucas's visits, which lessen the tension in the house. Meanwhile Jane receives a surprising letter from Miss Bingley, announcing the Netherfield party's sudden departure for London. She writes that she is hoping to see her brother engaged to Miss Darcy. Elizabeth is convinced of Bingley's affections for Jane and believes the move to be a plot entirely orchestrated by his sister. She tries to comfort Jane.

In **chapter twenty-two** Mr. Collins, after two days of Miss Lucas's show of sympathy, proposes to her. As a woman of little fortune with dwindling hopes of marriage, she accepts him. Elizabeth is shocked and saddened. Mrs. Bennet's surprise and resentment are extreme. More bad news comes in a second letter from Miss Bingley, who says that her brother will definitely stay in London all winter. Jane suffers through her mother's wonderment at this affront but tries to assure Elizabeth that she does not feel slighted.

In **chapter twenty-five** Elizabeth's uncle and aunt from London, Mr. and Mrs. Gardiner, arrive for Christmas. Elizabeth discusses Jane's affairs with Mrs. Gardiner, who is an intelligent, caring, and favorite relation. Jane is invited to return with the Gardiners to London. Before leaving, her aunt discusses Mr. Wickham with her niece. He is a favorite in town and since Darcy's departure has liberally advertised his grievances against his former patron's son. He has also continued to show a favoritism toward Elizabeth, and Mrs. Gardiner gently warns her against considering marriage to a man of no fortune.

Mr. Collins's wedding follows soon after the holidays. Elizabeth promises to visit Charlotte. Meanwhile Elizabeth hears from Jane in London. She writes of Miss Bingley's neglecting her notes and receiving her calls with the minimum of civility. At the same time, Elizabeth notices that Wickham's attentions have shifted to a less pretty woman who has just come into an inheritance of ten thousand pounds. Her disappointment is not excessive, but she nonetheless begins to look forward to a visit to the Collinses. In March she travels with Charlotte's sister and father, stopping overnight in London to see Jane. There her aunt criticizes Wickham's behavior.

The travelers continue to Hunsford and are greeted at the parsonage. Mr. Collins gleefully shows off his house and praises the adjoining de Bourgh estate of Rosings. Lady Catherine soon invites the party to dine. Elizabeth, on meeting this esteemed personage, is unimpressed by her snobbish, authoritative manner. Lady Catherine's daughter also turns out to be little more than a timid, sickly girl. After dinner her hostess grills Elizabeth on her upbringing, liberally criticizing what she hears. Elizabeth defends herself, making Lady Catherine exclaim with displeasure, "you give your opinions very decidedly for so young a person!"

After Elizabeth's first two quiet weeks at the parsonage, Mr. Darcy and his cousin Colonel Fitzwilliam come to visit their aunt. In **chapter thirty** Elizabeth meets Fitzwilliam, finding him a friendly, easy-mannered gentleman. He calls on her several times, but Darcy remains pointedly absent. The Collinses are eventually asked to dine at Rosings. There Elizabeth chats with the two cousins, playfully accusing Darcy of aloofness.

The next morning Darcy calls on the parsonage and finds Elizabeth alone (**chapter thirty-two**). An awkward conversation ensues in which Elizabeth questions Darcy about Bingley's sudden departure from Hertfordshire. Nothing is resolved, yet within the next several days Darcy, as well as his cousin, begins to call regularly at the parsonage. Elizabeth is puzzled by his visits, as he is often silent and uncomfortable. One day Elizabeth happens to meet Colonel Fitzwilliam in the park (**chapter thirty-three**). They speak of Bingley, and Fitzwilliam mentions that Darcy has recently saved him from an imprudent marriage. Elizabeth, recognizing her own family in his description, suppresses her indignation but is too upset to join the others for an evening at Rosings.

When her companions have left for dinner, Mr. Darcy unexpectedly calls (**chapter thirty-four**). Entering with unusual agitation, he abruptly declares his love to an astonished Elizabeth. He explains that he has struggled in vain against an attachment that would link him to an inferior family. Elizabeth counters by angrily refusing him. Darcy is shocked, thinking her acceptance assured, but Elizabeth censures him for his ungentlemanly behavior and accuses him of having ruined her sister's happiness and having destroyed the career of the noble Mr. Wickham. Darcy leaves in anger.

The next morning Elizabeth receives a long letter from Darcy (**chapter thirty-five**). He defends himself, describing his reservations about her family and explaining his belief that Jane had not been in love with Bingley. In the case of Mr. Wickham, he describes how this son of his father's steward had rejected his intended career of the church soon after the late Mr. Darcy's death. Instead he had demanded compensation for the bequeathed living in cash, which Darcy had given him. When the money had been gambled away, Wickham tried to improve his finances by eloping with Darcy's fifteen-year-old sister. Darcy had discovered the plot in time to save his sister from disgrace and had severed all ties with the ingrate.

Elizabeth finds Darcy's story difficult to believe, but as she reconsiders Wickham's behavior—his indiscretion in spreading his story and partiality toward heiresses—she begins to see the truth. In a painful moment of self-recognition, Austen's heroine realizes that her vanity and wounded pride have led her to judge undeservingly. "I who have prided myself on my discernment!" she exclaims. When, after hours of wandering the park lanes, she returns to the house, she finds that Darcy and Fitzwilliam have already left for London.

Elizabeth departs after another week's stay. She leaves still occupied with thoughts of Darcy. In London, Jane joins her on the trip back to Hertfordshire, where their two youngest sisters meet them at the inn. Elizabeth is newly disheartened by their silliness and poor manners.

At home Elizabeth tells Jane of Darcy's proposal and Wickham's dishonorable past (**chapter forty**). They decide to keep Wickham's character a secret because the militia is scheduled to leave in two weeks. Elizabeth does not tell Jane of Bingley's desertion, although Mrs. Bennet continues to harp on it. "My only comfort is," she concludes, "I am sure Jane will die of a broken heart, and then he will be sorry for what he has done."

The younger Bennet sisters despair over the militia's departure until Lydia is invited by one of the officer's wives to visit them in Brighton, the new station. Elizabeth secretly advises her father against Lydia's trip, but he lets her go. Once the militia has left, life returns to normal. Elizabeth looks forward to a summer trip to the north with Mr. and Mrs. Gardiner. At the last moment her uncle's plans change, and they find they can go only as far as Derbyshire, which is where Darcy has his estate. When they arrive in its vicinity, Mrs. Gardiner is eager to visit, and Elizabeth, who learns from a chambermaid that the master is not expected, reluctantly agrees.

In **chapter forty-three** Elizabeth visits the beautiful estate of Pemberley, of which she could have been mistress. The housekeeper who shows them around is sincere in her praise of Darcy as master and brother. As she is walking in the garden, Elizabeth's fears materialize when she spies Darcy walking nearby, having just arrived from London. He joins her, and she is surprised and embarrassed, but also astonished at his solicitous manners. Although her uncle is only a businessman, Darcy asks for an introduction and acts as a gracious host. Elizabeth learns that Miss Darcy and the Bingleys are to come the following day.

Punctually the next morning, Darcy brings his sister to call on Elizabeth (**chapter forty-four**). Miss Darcy is a reserved girl of sixteen who struggles against her shyness. Soon afterward, Mr. Bingley arrives to pay his respects. Elizabeth notices that he shows no affection for his friend's sister and still seems to think of Jane. After their visit Elizabeth spends the day puzzling over Darcy's alteration. Her own feelings toward him have changed from dislike to esteem and gratitude. The next day Elizabeth and Mrs. Gardiner call on Pemberley, where Miss Darcy greets them shyly while the Bingley sisters act false and cold. Darcy joins them, as solicitous as ever.

The next morning's post sadly disrupts their visit. In **chapter forty-six** a letter from Jane announces a terrible calamity: Lydia has eloped with Mr. Wickham. The couple do not seem to be married, and Mr. Bennet has gone to London to look for them. Just as Elizabeth finishes the letter, Darcy enters, finding her alone. Overcome with distress, she tells him the news. He is shocked and distracted, and after sending for her aunt and uncle soon departs. The three travelers then hastily return to the Bennet estate of Longbourn.

They find Mrs. Bennet prostrate with self-pity. No news has arrived from London. Mr. Gardiner leaves to join his brother-in-law, and the family waits under a shadow of disgrace. Meanwhile Wickham's reputation plummets in town, where it is discovered that he owes money to almost every local tradesman, as well as a thousand pounds in gambling debts incurred in Brighton. A letter of condolence arrives from Mr. Collins, who helpfully observes that "the death of your daughter would have been a blessing in comparison to this" and congratulates himself at not having married into the family. Mr. Bennet returns disheartened from London and admits to Elizabeth that he had been too lenient in Lydia's upbringing.

In **chapter forty-nine** news finally comes from Mr. Gardiner. He has found the couple, they are to be married, and Mr. Bennet is to pay only a small yearly allowance in return. Mr. Bennet worries that Mr. Gardiner has paid enormous sums to bribe Wickham into compliance. Mrs. Bennet, on the other hand, instantly recovers her health in the anticipation of the marriage. Meanwhile, Elizabeth realizes that all hope of marrying Darcy has been destroyed by her family's new connection to Wickham. She understands, now that all is lost, that Darcy is "the man who, in disposition and talents, would most suit her."

Her uncle finds Wickham a post in a regiment stationed far north, but before the newlyweds leave Elizabeth and Jane convince their father to allow them to visit. In **chapter fifty-one** Lydia descends on Longbourn on the day of her marriage giddily brandishing her wedding ring and oblivious to the suffering she has caused. Her two elder sisters are shocked, although her mother rejoices merrily. Elizabeth sadly observes Wickham's limited affection for Lydia.

Several days later Lydia describes her wedding to Elizabeth and lets slip that Darcy had been present. Elizabeth, astonished, writes to her aunt for an explanation. She learns in **chapter fifty-two** that Darcy had orchestrated the entire marriage. He had blamed himself for not making Wickham's true character known and had left Derbyshire for London the day after Elizabeth. He had located Wickham and convinced him to marry Lydia by offering him a large sum of money. He had then visited Mr. Gardiner and settled the matter. Elizabeth can only wonder at Darcy's generosity.

Meanwhile Lydia and her husband leave and Mrs. Bennet's spirits flag until she learns that Bingley plans to return for a few days of hunting. Jane assures Elizabeth of her indifference, but when Bingley comes to call Elizabeth sees that his admiration is rekindled. She is surprised that Darcy accompanies his friend and cringes at the jabs her mother directs at him while favoring Bingley. They all meet soon again at a dinner party, where Bingley continues to admire Jane and all Hertfordshire begins to speculate about their engagement. Elizabeth barely speaks to Darcy during the entire evening. In **chapter fifty-five** Darcy leaves for London and Bingley begins to call on the Bennets daily. Mrs. Bennet uses all her powers to get the lovers alone, and when she succeeds, Bingley promptly proposes. Jane consents, and the Bennets are "speedily pronounced the luckiest family in the world."

In the midst of their happiness, Lady Catherine arrives as a rude, haughty deus ex machina and demands an audience with Elizabeth. Elizabeth is astonished by her visit and even more surprised when, once they are alone, the distinguished woman accuses her of a secret engagement to Darcy. Elizabeth refuses to be bullied by her guest's intrusive questions, and Lady Catherine's irritation grows. "Miss Bennet, do you know who I am?" she demands, insisting that Darcy is to marry her own daughter. Elizabeth refuses to promise not to accept Darcy, and Lady Catherine leaves, "seriously displeased."

Several days later, Darcy returns and calls on Longbourn with Bingley (**chapter fifty-eight**). Elizabeth can no longer refrain from thanking him for what he has done for Lydia, and he tells her he has acted only out of concern for her. He then reveals his unaltered affections, and Elizabeth awkwardly explains her own change of heart. She learns that she can thank Lady Catherine for Darcy's second proposal. His aunt's report to Darcy of Elizabeth's impertinence gave him hope that she might accept him. Both lovers then, in a nod to the title, admit their faults. Elizabeth had been rash and thoughtless; Darcy, selfishly proud. He thanks her for the hard lesson she has taught him, saying, "I came to you without a doubt of my reception. You showed me how insufficient were all my pretensions to please a woman worthy of being pleased."

The next evening Darcy asks Mr. Bennet for Elizabeth's hand. Her father calls her to the library, troubled by Elizabeth's unexpected engagement, but is reassured of her sentiments. Bemused at the rapid series of betrothals, he tells Elizabeth, "If any young men come for Mary or Kitty, send them in, for I am quite at leisure." Mrs. Bennet is astonished to learn that "that disagreeable Mr. Darcy" is to be her son-in-law. The joy of his ten-thousand-pound income nearly drives her to distraction.

Thus two rocky courtships end happily. The drama of Austen's novel plays itself out on a small scale, with the most pressing crises being merely impediments to marriage. Her novel nonetheless reveals the depth of her subject, showing both the importance and risk of marriage within the strict confines of respectable society. An unhappy marriage is a burden a couple must endure for a lifetime. Mr. Bennet's unhappy choice has sentenced him to a life of absurdity and ironic complacence. Charlotte Lucas, who chooses to marry the inferior Mr. Collins rather than become an old maid, is cynical of marriage. She tells Elizabeth that courtships need not last long because "[h]appiness in marriage is entirely a matter of chance." Partners, no matter how similar they seem, "always continue to grow sufficiently unlike afterwards to have their share of vexation; and it is better to know as little as possible of the defects of the person with whom you are to pass your life." Darcy and Elizabeth's example disproves this maxim. They begin all too aware of each other's defects. When Darcy, despite his reservations, falls in love with Elizabeth and proposes, her angry rejection breaks them apart and forces them to recognize their own faults and reassess each other's virtues. Once they do become engaged, they have gained enough knowledge of each other to ensure a stable happiness. Even Jane and Bingley, who are less introspective, learn to value each other more because of their difficult, interrupted courtship. In contrast, the Collins's marriage seems far from ideal, and the most impulsive union of the novel, Lydia and Wickham's, is clearly unhappy.

On the other hand, a certain impulsive high-spiritedness is rewarded in Austen's world when it is practiced with wit and intelligence. The novel's message is, on a limited scale, democratic. Although Elizabeth is a gentleman's daughter, her family does not belong to the social class of the Darcys and de Bourghs. Nonetheless, her high spirits and resilience win her a husband who is her superior in wealth and rank. The marriage is happy, Austen shows, because she is his equal in sense and intelligence. ❖

*—Anna Guillemin*
*Princeton University*

# List of Characters

*Elizabeth Bennet* is the heroine of *Pride and Prejudice.* She is a witty, opinionated young woman whose disposition "delight[s] in any thing ridiculous." When the rich, aristocratic Mr. Darcy enters her social world as the friend of the town's new eligible bachelor, she finds him slightly ridiculous. His haughty demeanor and obvious disgust with provincial ways make her immediately dislike him. Elizabeth, as the second of five daughters from a middle-class landed family, has little to recommend herself to Mr. Darcy, but her unabashed, playful dismissal of him unwittingly kindles his admiration. When Darcy eventually proposes to Elizabeth, her pride is stung by his insistence on the social sacrifice he would make to marry her, and she angrily rejects him. She then learns that her judgment of his character had been based on vicious misinformation and blinded by her own prejudices. A series of misadventures make the chance of marriage seemingly impossible just as Elizabeth finds herself falling in love with Darcy. Ironically, a final instance of Elizabeth's nettled pride prompts a second proposal, which she happily accepts.

*Mr. Darcy* is the proud, aristocratic gentleman who falls in love with the socially inferior Miss Bennet and must overcome his reservations about her family to marry her. He is an independent gentleman with an income of ten thousand pounds a year and a beautiful estate in Derbyshire, England. As a guest of Mr. Bingley, the newly established bachelor at Hertfordshire, he does not share his friend's enthusiasm for the unsophisticated provincial lifestyle. He worries about his friend's admiration of the eldest Miss Bennet, Jane, while unwittingly falling in love with her sister Elizabeth. While he dissuades Bingley from continuing to court Jane, he finds, on meeting Elizabeth again, that he is too deeply in love, and proposes. Darcy is shocked and sobered by Elizabeth's rejection. When he next meets her, he tries to reform his manners and then secretly helps her family in a moment of grave social crisis. When he learns that Elizabeth has changed her opinion of him, he proposes again and is happily accepted.

*Mr. Wickham* is the closest approximation to a villain in Austen's novel of social mores. He is a dashing young lieutenant who spreads vicious rumors about Darcy. His father had been the late Mr. Darcy's steward. He claims to Elizabeth that the present Mr. Darcy had dishonorably ignored his father's will and turned Wickham out penniless. Wickham's charms temporarily attract Elizabeth, but she learns from Darcy that his stories are lies. Wickham had actually tried to elope with Darcy's younger sister to procure her inheritance. Wickham's true self emerges when he successfully elopes with Elizabeth's younger sister, leaving a thousand pounds in gambling debts. Only Darcy's secret intervention bribes him into marrying Lydia Bennet and saving the family from disgrace.

*Jane Bennet* is Elizabeth's beautiful and sweet-natured older sister. The two are friends and confidants. Jane, who falls in love with the equally open, good-natured Mr. Bingley, suffers under her mother's premature, enthusiastic hints about an impending marriage. She does not see as clearly as Elizabeth how her family's ill breeding disgusts Bingley's friends. When Bingley hastily leaves Hertfordshire, Jane suffers quietly, but her story ends happily when he returns some ten months later to declare his love.

*Mr. Bingley* is the eligible young bachelor with an income of five thousand pounds a year whose arrival at Hertfordshire sends the female population into a flurry of excitement. He soon falls in love with Jane Bennet but is dissuaded by his snobbish sister and concerned friend Darcy from pursuing the courtship. After a separation of some ten months he returns and, with Darcy's newfound approval, proposes to Jane.

*Mr. Bennet* is the wry and sarcastic father of the five Bennet daughters and husband of a very silly wife. He suffers through their enthusiasms and hysterics with a certain bemused detachment. Elizabeth, who shares his critical sensibilities, is his favorite. He is chastened by Lydia's elopement and realizes that a more disciplined upbringing could have prevented his daughter's thoughtless behavior.

*Mrs. Bennet* is one of the more caricatured of Austen's creations. She is a silly, self-centered woman who unfailingly exposes her senselessness while trying to impress her daughters' suitors. Her one goal in life is to find husbands for her five offspring, but her lack of refinement and subtlety does much to hamstring her projects.

*Mr. Collins* is Mr. Bennet's dull and obsequious cousin who is to inherit the family's estate of Longbourn. He is rector in the parish of Lady Catherine de Bourgh, Darcy's aunt. He visits the Bennets and soon pompously proposes to Elizabeth, who refuses him. Spurned, he then almost immediately becomes engaged to Elizabeth's close friend. Mr. Collins reenters the story as Elizabeth's tedious host when she visits the newlyweds some months later and meets Darcy again.

*Miss Bingley* is Mr. Bingley's sister, an example of an elegant, superficial upper-class lady. She comes to live with her brother and befriends Jane Bennet for lack of better company but actively prevents her engagement to Bingley. Meanwhile, she herself pursues rich Mr. Darcy and turns livid with jealousy watching his growing attachment to Elizabeth.

*Lydia Bennet* is the youngest of the Bennet sisters. She is her mother's favorite and, at the age of fifteen, already a seasoned flirt. Jane and Elizabeth suffer through her giddy misbehavior at local gatherings, which attracts the silent censure of Darcy and Miss Bingley, but the real crisis comes when Lydia, while staying with a friend in Brighton, elopes with Wickham. Belatedly married, she returns for a visit as wild and giddy as ever.

*Lady Catherine de Bourgh* is Darcy's aristocratic aunt and Mr. Collins's esteemed patroness. When Elizabeth meets this highly praised personage, she is surprised to find a petty, arrogant woman. Lady Catherine, who slights the Collins's guests while doting on her beloved Darcy, proves that ill breeding runs throughout class lines. She cherishes the idea of Darcy marrying her frail, ugly daughter. When she hears a false rumor that Darcy is engaged to Elizabeth, she descends on Longbourn to break off the alliance. Her trip has the opposite effect. Her rude condescension causes Elizabeth to say things that, when reported to Darcy, make him return and propose. ❖

# Critical Views

[Jane Austen was pleased with the appearance of *Pride and Prejudice* and generally satisfied with the substance of the novel. In letters to her sister Cassandra, Austen takes pride in the character of Elizabeth Bennet but wonders whether the work as a whole is perhaps too light and frivolous.]

Miss Benn dined with us on the very day of the books coming & in the evening we set fairly at it, and read half the first vol. to her, prefacing that, having intelligence from Henry that such a work would soon appear, we had desired him to send it whenever it came out, and I believe it passed with her unsuspected. She was amused, poor soul! *That* she could not help, you know, with two such people to lead the way, but she really does seem to admire Elizabeth. I must confess that I think her as delightful a creature as ever appeared in print, and how I shall be able to tolerate those who do not like *her* at least I do not know.

⟨. . .⟩ Our second evening's reading to Miss Benn had not pleased me so well, but I believe something must be attributed to my mother's too rapid way of getting on: and though she perfectly understands the characters herself, she cannot speak as they ought. Upon the whole, however, I am quite vain enough and well satisfied enough. The work is rather too light, and bright, and sparkling; it wants shade; it wants to be stretched out here and there with a long chapter of sense, if it could be had; if not, of solemn specious nonsense, about something unconnected with the story; an essay on writing, a critique on Walter Scott, or the history of Buonaparté, or anything that would form a contrast, and bring the reader with increased delight to the playfulness and epigrammatism of the general style.

> —Jane Austen, Letters to Cassandra Austen (29 January and 4 February 1813), *Letters to Her Sister Cassandra and Others,* ed. R. W. Chapman (London: Oxford University Press, 1932), pp. 297–300

❖

[Mary Russell Mitford (1787–1855) was a well-known poet, dramatist, and novelist of the period, best known for *Our Village* (1832), a series of sketches of rural life. In this letter, Mitford praises Austen but finds that her female characters lack "grace" or "taste."]

The want of elegance is almost the only want in Miss Austen. I have not read her *Mansfield Park;* but it is impossible not to feel in every line of *Pride and Prejudice,* in every word of Elizabeth, the entire want of taste which could produce so pert, so worldly a heroine as the beloved of such a man as Darcy. Wickham is equally bad. Oh! they were just fit for each other, and I cannot forgive that delightful Darcy for parting them. Darcy should have married Jane. He is of all the admirable characters the best designed and the best sustained. I quite agree with you in preferring Miss Austen to Miss Edgeworth. If the former had a little more taste, a little more perception of the graceful, as well as of the humorous, I know not indeed any one to whom I should not prefer her. There is none of the hardness, the cold selfishness, of Miss Edgeworth about her writings; she is in a much better humour with the world; she preaches no sermons; she wants nothing but the *beau idéal* of the female character to be a perfect novel-writer; and perhaps even that *beau idéal* would only be missed by such a *petite maîtresse* in books as myself, who would never admit a muse into my library till she had been taught to dance by the Graces.

—Mary Russell Mitford, Letter to Sir William Elford (20 December 1814), *The Letters of Mary Russell Mitford,* ed. R. Brimley Johnson (New York: Dial Press, 1925), pp. 121–22

❖

## Sir Walter Scott on Austen's Ability to Portray Ordinary Life

[Sir Walter Scott (1771–1832) was one of the greatest historical novelists in literary history and also a prolific critic and essayist. In this extract from his journal, Scott finds Austen's greatest skill to reside in her power to portray vividly the commonplace activities of life.]

Also read again and for the third time at least Miss Austen's very finely written novel of *Pride and Prejudice*. That young lady had a talent for describing the involvements and feelings and characters of ordinary life which is to me the most wonderful I ever met with. The Big Bow-wow strain I can do myself like any now going, but the exquisite touch which renders ordinary commonplace things and characters interesting from the truth of the description and the sentiment is denied to me. What a pity such a gifted creature died so early!
—Sir Walter Scott, *Journal* (14 March 1826), *The Journal of Sir Walter Scott* (Edinburgh: Oliver & Boyd, 1950), p. 135

❖

## Charlotte Brontë on Austen's Limited Range

[Charlotte Brontë (1816–1855) was the celebrated author of *Jane Eyre* (1847) and other novels. In this celebrated extract from a letter, Brontë—many of whose own works are set in the wilds of Yorkshire—criticizes Austen for the apparently limited range of *Pride and Prejudice* and its excessively restrained style.]

Why do you like Miss Austen so very much? I am puzzled on that point. What induced you to say that you would have rather written *Pride and Prejudice* or *Tom Jones*, than any of the Waverley Novels?

I had not seen *Pride and Prejudice* till I read that sentence of yours, and then I got the book. And what did I find? An accurate daguerreotyped portrait of a commonplace face; a carefully fenced, highly cultivated garden, with neat borders and delicate flowers; but no glance of a bright, vivid physiognomy, no open country, no fresh air, no blue hill, no bonny beck. I should hardly like to live with her ladies and gentlemen, in their elegant but confined houses.

—Charlotte Brontë, Letter to George Henry Lewes (12 January 1848), *The Letters of the Brontës: A Selection,* ed. Muriel Spark (Norman: University of Oklahoma Press, 1954), p. 143

❖

## WILBUR L. CROSS ON ELIZABETH'S PREJUDICE

[Wilbur L. Cross (1862–1948), a journalist, critic, and editor, is the author of *The Works and Life of Laurence Sterne* (1904), *Four Contemporary Novelists* (1930), and *The Development of the English Novel* (1899), a well-known study from which the following extract is taken. Here, Cross focuses on the Shakespearean way in which Austen portrays Elizabeth Bennet's prejudice against Darcy and its gradual dissipation.]

*Pride and Prejudice* has not only the humor of Shakespearean comedy, but also its technique. Elizabeth first meets Darcy at a village ball. She at once becomes prejudiced against him on account of the general *hauteur* of his bearing toward the village girls, and especially on account of a remark of his to his friend Bingley, which she overhears—a remark to the effect that, though she is tolerable, she is not handsome enough to tempt him to dance with her. Jane Austen now displays very great skill in handling events to the deepening of Elizabeth's prejudice, and to the awakening of Darcy's love, in spite of his pride. When prejudice and proud love have reached the proper degree of intensity, she brings Elizabeth and Darcy together at the Hunsford Parsonage; there is an arrogant and insulting proposal of marriage and an indignant refusal. From this scene on to the end of her story, Jane Austen is at her very best. By easy gradations, through a process of disillusioning, Elizabeth's prejudice vanishes, and with its gradual vanishing goes on the almost pitiable humiliation of Darcy. The marriage of Elizabeth and Darcy is not merely a possible solution of the plot, it is as inevitable as the conclusion of a properly constructed syllogism or geometrical demonstration. For a parallel to workmanship of this high order, one can look only to Shakespeare, to such a comedy as *Much Ado about Nothing.*

—Wilbur L. Cross, *The Development of the English Novel* (London: Macmillan, 1899), pp. 119–20

❖

## MARY LASCELLES ON THE MUTUAL MISUNDERSTANDING OF ELIZABETH AND DARCY

[Mary Lascelles, a noted British critic, is the author of *Nations and Facts: Collected Criticism and Research* (1972), *The Story-teller Retrieves the Past* (1980), and other volumes. In this extract from her book on Austen, Lascelles praises Austen's use of circumstance and supporting characters in driving Elizabeth's and Darcy's mutual misunderstanding forward until its climax is reached.]

Elizabeth's chief impetus is due to Wickham; but there is hardly a character in the story who contributes no momentum to it, nor any pressure from without to which she does not respond characteristically. Her misunderstanding of Darcy is thus much less simple, much less like the given condition of an invented problem, than Marianne's misunderstanding of Willoughby, or of Elinor. Her initial impulse towards this misunderstanding comes, of course, from Darcy himself, in that piece of flamboyant rudeness which I suspect of being a little out of keeping; but from this point on all follows plausibly. Darcy's more characteristic reference to his own implacability prepares her to believe just what she is going to hear of him so soon as Wickham addresses her. And how insinuating that address is! There had been a suspicion of burlesque about Willoughby's mode of entrance into the story—something that recalls the ironic apology for the absence of the hero in the opening of *Northanger Abbey;* chance has disposed it too smoothly to his advantage. Wickham owes no more to chance than that first silent encounter with Darcy that stirs Elizabeth's wakeful curiosity; it is his adroitness that transforms curiosity into sympathetic indignation. What provincial young lady, brought up among the small mysteries and intrigues of Mrs. Bennet's world, would not be flattered into sympathy by his relation of his own story (so nicely corresponding with that of many heroes in popular fiction), or would criticize him for telling or herself for listening to such a private history? Or what young lady of Elizabeth's self-assurance would suspect that she was not to remain its only hearer? Henceforward his adversaries—and even indifferent spectators—play into his hands: Miss Bingley's insolent interference rouses Elizabeth's pride and clouds her judgement; Charlotte Lucas causes her to mistake her own prejudice for generous sentiment; Mr. Collins, by associating Darcy in her mind with the idol of his worship, strengthens every ill impression; Lady Catherine herself, by answering to Wickham's description, confirms part of his story, and by her proprietary praise of Darcy fixes some of its implications; and Colonel Fitzwilliam, by his indiscreet half-confidence, ensures that Elizabeth shall see Darcy's action towards her sister in the harshest light.

Meanwhile, Darcy's ill opinion of the Bennets has been growing, under the influence of these very people and events, until the climax of the ungracious proposal and refusal is reached. And yet, in the centre of this disturbance, forces have begun to stir, and, almost imperceptibly, to allay it. And this entails a change of course which is very difficult to contrive. The initial impulse must not seem to have spent itself—that would leave a fatal impression of lassitude. There must be deflexion; and this, for Jane Austen, means cause and opportunity to reconsider character and action. (Not conduct alone; she has little use for those casual encounters in ambiguous circumstances which are the staple of Fanny Burney's misunderstandings between lovers.) Even while they are drawing yet farther apart, Elizabeth and Darcy have begun to feel unfamiliar

doubts; sure as each still is of his and her own critical judgement, both have come to question the standards of their own
social worlds. Her mother's behaviour at Netherfield on two
uncomfortable occasions disturbs Elizabeth in such a way as to
suggest that she had not been embarrassed by it before; and
Charlotte Lucas's conduct shocks her. Presently, Colonel
Fitzwilliam's manners give her a standard by which to judge
Wickham's. In the meantime Darcy has been unwillingly learning to criticize the manners of his world as it is represented by
Miss Bingley, and—touching him more smartly—by Lady
Catherine.

> 'I have told Miss Bennet several times, that she will never play
> really well, unless she practises more; and though Mrs. Collins
> has no instrument, she is very welcome, as I have often told her,
> to come to Rosings every day, and play on the piano forte in
> Mrs. Jenkinson's room. She would be in nobody's way, you
> know, in that part of the house.' Mr. Darcy looked a little
> ashamed of his aunt's ill breeding, and made no answer.

And so, even when the climax of mutual exasperation is
reached, Elizabeth's criticism of Darcy meets some response in
his consciousness, his statement of his objections to her family
means something to her; and the way is open for each to consider anew the actions and character of the other. What Darcy
has done is now shown afresh in his letter; this I do not find
quite plausible. The manner is right, but not the matter: so
much, and such, information would hardly be volunteered by a
proud and reserved man—unless under pressure from his
author, anxious to get on with the story. And perhaps it may
be the same pressure that hastens Elizabeth's complete acceptance of its witness; for there is no time to lose; she must have
revised her whole impression of him before her visit to
Pemberley—revised it confidently enough to be able to indi-
cate as much clearly to Wickham, for our benefit: 'I think', she
says enigmatically in answer to his searching questions, 'Mr.
Darcy improves on acquaintance.' This disturbs and provokes
him to further inquiry: ' "For I dare not hope," he continued in a
lower and more serious tone, "that he is improved in essentials." "Oh, no!" said Elizabeth. "In essentials, I believe, he is

very much what he ever was" '—and she develops this proposition to Wickham's discomfort.

—Mary Lascelles, *Jane Austen and Her Art* (Oxford: Clarendon Press, 1939), pp. 160–63

❖

## R. W. CHAPMAN ON AUSTEN'S ECONOMY

[R. W. Chapman (1881–1960), a distinguished British critic and editor, produced editions of the works of Jane Austen and of Samuel Johnson's letters and wrote *Jane Austen: Facts and Problems* (1948), from which the following extract is taken. Here, Chapman comments on the limitations of Austen's delineation of Darcy.]

I will pivot on *Pride and Prejudice* a note on one aspect of Jane Austen's economy: her rigid avoidance of anything outside her experience or her chosen subject. It has been noted that she hardly ever leaves two of her young men alone together. She did not know just what they would say. This is, of course, a limitation, indeed a serious one. But she was a woman, belonging to a strict sect of the upper middle class; she had not the opportunities of a George Eliot. Nor had she that power of divination which allowed Trollope to follow young women to a common bedroom—or at least as far as the keyhole—and report their talk. But a limitation, if by circumstance or by nature it is ineluctable, should be obeyed, not evaded; and Jane Austen's dexterity is such that the disadvantage is hardly perceived. She knew enough of her young men for her own purpose, and perhaps rather more than the girls did who were to marry them.

So, in *Pride and Prejudice,* we see Darcy at a ball; on a visit to his friend and his friend's sisters, or to his noble aunt; calling at Hunsford parsonage. His more masculine or more public activities are merely reported, oftener merely hinted. But I think we can, by a legitimate use of the imagination, get a glimpse of these activities. We can see him, for instance, in his library, of which he could not conceive the neglect 'in times like these'; walking in the grounds of Pemberley, dispensing orders and charity; in Bingley's picture of him as an 'awful object . . . at his own house . . . of a Sunday evening when he has nothing to do'. His name, Fitzwilliam Darcy, his mother's, Lady Anne, and the grandeurs of Pemberley, identify him as a Northern magnate at a time when territorial influence, especially in the wide spaces of the North, was still all-powerful. I find it easy to jump a few hurdles and to see him as a public character: answering an invitation to stand for the county, or dining with the Archbishop of York.

Jane Austen's letters tell us a good deal of this her 'own darling child', which we may believe remained her favourite when she had moved on to more serious or more ambitious work. They give only one glimpse of her hero, which I cannot resist, though it has already been mentioned. She went to an exhibition in London, and was disappointed to find no portrait of Elizabeth. She could only suppose that Darcy would not allow it to be 'exposed to the public eye. I can imagine he would have that sort of feeling—that mixture of Love, Pride, and Delicacy.' This is a good illustration of Jane Austen's habit (the records are tantalizing) of letting her imagination work—but not for publication—outside the frame of her picture. It gives moreover a pleasing instance of the 'proper' pride to which Elizabeth's influence had confined her lover and husband.

 —R. W. Chapman, *Jane Austen: Facts and Problems* (Oxford: Clarendon Press, 1948), pp. 187–89

❧

## REUBEN ARTHUR BROWER ON AUSTEN'S WIT

[Reuben Arthur Brower (1908–1975) taught English at Harvard University and lectured at many other schools. His publications include *Alexander Pope: The Poetry of Allusion* (1959), *In Defense of Reading* (1962), and *Hero and Saint: Shakespeare and the Graeco-Roman Heroic Tradition* (1971). In this extract, Brower compares Austen's wit to Pope's and notes her success in showing a convincing "change of sentiment."]

Many pages of *Pride and Prejudice* can be read as sheer poetry of wit, as Pope without couplets. The antitheses are almost as frequent and almost as varied; the play of ambiguities is certainly as complex; the orchestration of tones is as precise and subtle. As in the best of Pope, the displays of ironic wit are not without imaginative connection; what looks most diverse is really most similar, and ironies are linked by vibrant reference to basic certainties. There are passages too in which the rhythmical pattern of the sentence approaches the formal balance of the heroic couplet:

> Mr. Bennet was so odd a mixture of quick parts, sarcastic humour, reserve, and caprice, that the experience of three and twenty years had been insufficient to make his wife understand his character. *Her* mind was less difficult to develope. She was a woman of mean understanding, little information, and uncertain temper. When she was discontented she fancied herself nervous. The business of her life was to get her daughters married; its solace was visiting and news.

The triumph of the novel—whatever its limitations may be—lies in combining such poetry of wit with the dramatic structure of fiction. In historical terms, to combine the traditions of poetic satire with those of the sentimental novel, that was Jane Austen's feat in *Pride and Prejudice.*

For the 'bright and sparkling,' seemingly centrifugal play of irony is dramatically functional. It makes sense as literary art, the sense with which a writer is most concerned. The repartee, while constantly amusing, delineates characters and their changing relations and points the way to a climactic moment in which the change is most clearly recognized. Strictly speaking, this union of wit and drama is achieved with complete success only in the central sequence of *Pride and Prejudice,* in the presentation of Elizabeth's and Darcy's gradual revaluation of each other. Here, if anywhere, Jane Austen met James's demand that the novel should give its readers the maximum of 'fun'; at the same time she satisfied the further standard implied in James's remark that the art of the novel is 'above all an art of preparations.' That she met these demands more continuously in

*Emma* does not detract from her achievement in *Pride and Prejudice.*⟨. . .⟩

The triumph of *Pride and Prejudice* is a rare one, just because it is so difficult to balance a purely ironic vision with credible presentation of a man and woman undergoing a serious 'change of sentiment.' Shakespeare achieves an uneasy success in *Much Ado About Nothing,* and Fielding succeeds in *Tom Jones* because he does not expect us to take 'love' too seriously. The problem for the writer who essays this difficult blend is one of creating dramatic speech which fulfils his complex intention. In solving this problem of expression, Jane Austen has her special triumph.

> —Reuben Arthur Brower, "Light and Bright and Sparkling: Irony and Fiction in *Pride and Prejudice,*" *The Fields of Light: An Experiment in Critical Reading* (New York: Oxford University Press, 1951), pp. 164–65, 181

❖

## MARVIN MUDRICK ON THE INDIVIDUAL IN A RESTRICTIVE SOCIAL FRAMEWORK

[Marvin Mudrick (b. 1921) is a former professor of English at the University of California at Santa Barbara and author of *Books Are Not Life, But Then, What Is?* (1979) and *Nobody Here But Us Children* (1981). In this extract from his book on Austen, Mudrick explores the complicated world of social restrictions in *Pride and Prejudice* and points out that the story still centers on Elizabeth's power to choose her own destiny.]

The central fact for Elizabeth remains the power of choice. In spite of social pressures, in spite of the misunderstandings and the obstacles to awareness that cut off and confuse the individual, in spite of the individual's repeated failures, the power of choice is all that distinguishes him as a being who acts and who may be judged. There are, certainly, limitations upon his choice, the limitations of an imposed prudence, of living within a social frame in which material comfort is an article of prestige and a sign of moral well-being: since even Elizabeth, though an acute and critical observer, is no rebel, she cannot contemplate the possibility of happiness outside her given social frame. The author is, likewise, pointedly ironic in contrasting Elizabeth's charitable allowances, first for Wickham, and then for Colonel Fitzwilliam, an "Earl's younger son," when her relative poverty obliges them to regard her as ineligible. Yet the irony does not go so far as to invalidate choice or distinctions in choice. Fitzwilliam, no rebel, is prudent in the hope that both prudence and inclination may be satisfied together in the future; but Wickham's "prudence," rather than merely limiting his choice, has deprived him of it entirely. In Elizabeth's feeling, upon touring Darcy's estate, "that to be mistress of Pemberley might be something!" the irony is circumscribed with an equal clarity: Darcy gains by being a rich man with a magnificent estate; but Pemberley is an expression of Darcy's taste as well as of his wealth and rank, and the image of Pemberley cannot divert Elizabeth from her primary concern with Darcy's motives and the meaning of his façade. Pemberley with Mr. Collins, or even with Bingley, would not do at all.

The focus is upon the complex individual; the only quality that distinguishes him from his setting, from the forms of courtship and marriage in an acquisitive society, which other-wise standardize and absorb him, is also his unique function—choice. What Elizabeth must choose, within the bounds set by prudence, is an individual equally complex, and undefeated by his social role. The complex individual is, after all, isolated by his freedom, and must be seen so at the end; for even if pressures from without, from the social system and the social class, deflect or overwhelm him, they demonstrate not that he is indistinguishable from his social role, but that he is vulnerable to it. The fact of choice makes him stand, finally, alone, to judge or be judged.

—Marvin Mudrick, Jane Austen: Irony as Defense and Discovery<br>(Princeton University Press, 1952), pp. 124–25

❖

[Dorothy Van Ghent (b. 1907) is the author of *Willa
Cather* (1964), *Keats: The Myth of the Hero* (1983), and
*The English Novel: Form and Function* (1953), from
which the following extract is taken. Here, Van Ghent
believes that the limited scope of Austen's novels is
not due to ignorance of the harsher realities of life but
to a deliberate artistic decision.]

It is the frequent response of readers who are making their first
acquaintance with Jane Austen that her subject matter is itself
so limited—limited to the manners of a small section of English
country gentry who apparently never have been worried about
death or sex, hunger or war, guilt or God—that it can offer no
contiguity with modern interests. This is a very real difficulty in
an approach to an Austen novel, and we should not obscure it;
for by taking it initially into consideration, we can begin to
come closer to the actual toughness and subtlety of the Austen
quality. The greatest novels have been great in range as well as
in technical invention; they have explored human experience a
good deal more widely and deeply than Jane Austen was able
to explore it. It is wronging an Austen novel to expect of it
what it makes no pretense to rival—the spiritual profundity of
the very greatest novels. But if we expect artistic mastery of
limited materials, we shall not be disappointed.

The exclusions and limitations are deliberate; they do not
necessarily represent limitations of Jane Austen's personal
experience. Though she led the life of a maiden gentlewoman,
it was not actually a sheltered life—not sheltered, that is, from
the apparition of a number of the harsher human difficulties.
She was a member of a large family whose activities ramified in
many directions, in a period when a cousin could be guil-
lotined, when an aunt and uncle could be jailed for a year on a
shopkeeper's petty falsification, and when the pregnancies and
childbed mortalities of relatives and friends were kept up at a
barnyard rate. Her letters show in her the ironical mentality and
the eighteenth-century gusto that are the reverse of the puri-
tanism and naïveté that might be associated with the maidenly

life. What she excludes from her fictional material does not, then, reflect a personal obliviousness, but, rather, a critically developed knowledge of the character of her gift and a restriction of its exercise to the kind of subject matter which she could shape into most significance. When we begin to look upon these limitations, not as having the negative function of showing how much of human life Jane Austen left out, but as having, rather, the positive function of defining the form and meaning of the book, we begin also to understand that kind of value that can lie in artistic mastery over a restricted range. This "two inches of ivory" (the metaphor which she herself used to describe her work), though it may resemble the handle of a lady's fan when looked on scantly, is in substance an elephant's tusk; it is a savagely probing instrument as well as a masterpiece of refinement.

—Dorothy Van Ghent, "On *Pride and Prejudice,*" *The English Novel: Form and Function* (New York: Holt, Rinehart & Winston, 1953), pp. 99–100

❖

DAVID DAICHES ON THE SOCIAL HIERARCHY IN *PRIDE AND PREJUDICE*

[David Daiches (b. 1912) is a prolific Scottish literary critic. He is a professor of English and director of graduate studies at the University of Edinburgh and the author of many books, including *The Novel and the Modern World* (1960) and *Literature and Society* (1969). In this extract, Daiches examines the social hierarchy in *Pride and Prejudice* and concludes that Austen accepted the class distinctions present in her day.]

The problem posed in what might be called the first movement of the novel is the marrying off of the elder Bennet girls. They have beauty and intelligence, but (thanks to the entail so deplored by Mrs. Bennet) inconsiderable fortune. Mrs. Bennet's desire to have them married, though her expression of that desire reveals the defects of her character in a richly comic manner, is itself both natural and laudable; for girls of negligible fortune genteelly brought up must secure their man while they may, or face a precarious shabby-genteel spinsterhood with few opportunities of personal satisfaction or social esteem. The problem as originally posed has its comic side, but the arrival of Mr. Collins (though he himself is a highly comic figure) shows it in another light.

Mr. Collins is a kind of grotesque, who takes his place in the stately ballet of social life with fantastic *gaucherie.* By his proposal to Elizabeth (again, a richly comic incident in itself) he points up another side of the marriage-seeking business: economic security can be won at too great a cost. When Elizabeth's friend Charlotte Lucas accepts Mr. Collins, we are for the first time made fully aware of some of the ugly realities underlying the stately social ballet. It is a dance on the sunlit grass, but some of the dancers at least are in earnest, and if they do not secure a permanent partner before the end of the day they will be left alone for ever on the dark and deserted lawn, or forced to find refuge in the pathless woods which surround the trimly kept grass plot. Rather than face such a fate—rather, that is, than be left with no prospect of social or economic security in an age when few means of earning an independent livelihood were open to the daughters of gentlemen—Charlotte Lucas, an intelligent girl who enjoys the friendship of such a discriminating person as Elizabeth, marries the grotesque Mr. Collins. She knows it is her last chance, and she takes it deliberately, weighing her future husband's intolerable character against the security and social position he offers. Elizabeth is shocked, but Jane Austen takes some pains to let her readers know how hopeless the choice was, and how in fact Charlotte has chosen the lesser of two evils. ⟨. . .⟩

In the gradual unfolding of the truth about Darcy's character in *Pride and Prejudice,* the revelation of his goodness to his tenants and in general of his playing the part of the landowner who understands the social duties that ownership implies (we see this in the housekeeper's talk to Elizabeth and her aunt and uncle at Pemberley) represents a crucial stage. Jane Austen had a strong sense of class duty and a contempt for any claims for superiority based merely on noble birth or social snobbery.

Lady Catherine de Bourgh is a monstrous caricature of Darcy: she represents pride without intelligence, moral sense, or understanding of the obligations conferred by rank. Jane Austen of course accepts the class structure of English society as she knew it; but she accepts it as a type of human society, in which privilege implies duty. Her view of life is both moral and hierarchical. But it is far from snobbish, if by snobbery we mean the admiration of rank or social position as such.

—David Daiches, A Critical History of English Literature (New York: Ronald Press, 1960), Vol. 2, pp. 751–52, 754

❖

### ROBERT LIDDELL ON WICKHAM AS ANTI-HERO

[Robert Liddell (1908–1992) was the head of the department of English at the University of Athens and a British Council lecturer in Greece. His publications include *A Treatise on the Novel* (1947), *Cavafy: A Critical Biography* (1974), and *The Novels of George Eliot* (1977). In this extract from his book on Austen, Liddell explores the function of Wickham as an anti-hero in *Pride and Prejudice*.]

Of all the anti-heroes, Wickham is the most odious. It is, indeed, almost as remarkable that Elizabeth should attach herself to him, as that Emma should propose Mr Elton as an elegant husband for Harriet. They are both underbred, and in Wickham's case we are allowed to suppose that an extravagant and pretentious mother had counteracted the excellent education with which his godfather, Mr George Darcy, had provided him. It is, of course, possible to find explanations: it is known that women often have bad taste in men (as men in women). Neither Elizabeth nor Emma has seen much of the world; Elizabeth is misled by her shrewdness, and Emma (who is a particularly poor judge of character) has a great belief in her judgement. Nevertheless, the improbability should have been done away; not the least improbable thing is that these two flashy men should fail, for quite a number of chapters, to show themselves in their worst colours. For ill-breeding cannot be dissembled, like a vice, and flashiness has no wish to dissemble. It is not only Elizabeth who thinks Wickham charming.

As a liar, he is indeed extremely plausible, clever enough to tell a great deal of truth, and to exploit a situation where all the sympathy will be on his side. In life, or on the stage, his 'countenance' might speak for him; I think his creator forgets that it can do nothing for him between the covers of a book, and that she ought, in some way, to have made it up to him.

On his elopement with Lydia, Jane Austen has simply failed (or declined) to use her imagination—as on Henry Crawford's with Maria Rushworth. Henry went off with her 'because he could not help it'—which is absurd enough, but there had been trouble brewing with old Mrs Rushworth and her threatening maid. The best explanation Elizabeth can give herself (or us) of Wickham's conduct is that 'his flight was rendered necessary by distress of circumstances; and if that were the case, he was not the young man to resist an opportunity of having a companion.' But a young man in distressed circumstances, who is fleeing them, and hoping to retrieve himself by a mercenary marriage in some other part of the country, is hardly likely to choose that moment to burden himself with a mistress for whom he has no great feeling. Maria Rushworth might be difficult to shake off, and Henry Crawford had the instincts of a gentleman; Lydia Bennet would not have presented the same problem, and Wickham was inhibited by no such instincts.

—Robert Liddell, *The Novels of Jane Austen* (London: Longmans, 1963), pp. 54–55

❖

YASMINE GOONERATNE ON THE FIRST LINE OF *PRIDE AND PREJUDICE*

[Yasmine Gooneratne (b. 1935) is a professor of English at Macquarie University in Australia and the director of the Post-Colonial Literature and Language Research

Centre. She is the author of *Alexander Pope* (1976) and *Diverse Literature: A Personal Perspective on Commonwealth Literature* (1980). In this extract from her book on Austen, Gooneratne examines the first line of *Pride and Prejudice,* showing how it establishes the tone and moral argument of the work.]

Consider the opening sentence of *Pride and Prejudice:*

> It is a truth universally acknowledged, that a single man in possession of a good fortune, must be in want of a wife.

In the first six words Jane Austen appears to state a fact that her use of the word *truth* implies to be a principle: a moral truth with which all mankind can be reasonably expected to agree. And what is this universally acknowledged principle? That a good income in the hands of a bachelor suffices in itself to make an attractive matrimonial proposition of him! The *tone,* which is dignified, oracular, elevated—as befits a person uttering edifying moral truths—has to keep uneasy company with *factual material* that savours of the cattle market rather than of religion or of philosophy. The crudeness of the idea expressed so simply in the second part of the sentence surprises the reader by its unexpectedness, after such a dignified beginning. It rouses, then amuses him. At the same time, the opening phrase casts some of its own dignity over that crudity of sentiment, reminding the reader that this attitude to marriage has the influence of a religious maxim with a great many people: it is 'universally acknowledged.' Jane Austen holds up for examination in this way, society's tendency to place a price, quite blatantly and complacently, on an intimate human relationship such as marriage. With its implicit protest at a corrupt social morality, her opening sentence sets out one of the novel's major themes, and hints at Elizabeth Bennet's coming struggle to preserve her personality from socially countenanced attack and exploitation by her elders and social superiors.

Writing of this kind, whether in the comparatively simple form of Emma Watson's reply to Lord Osborne or in the complex narrative of *Pride and Prejudice,* is not within the range of a careless or a slovenly writer because it depends for its effects on exactness and precision. Irony becomes more than a sharp retort in dialogue, to be resorted to (as Emma Watson does)

when politeness has failed: it becomes the stuff from which the novels are fashioned. Jane Austen's narration of incident and action, her portrayal of character, her management of dialogue—all these are conceived on two levels, how people present themselves to the world, and what they really are. As she matures, her characteristically ironic vision takes in landscape and environment as well, and an ever-widening range of human activity. The settings of the novels begin increasingly to participate in the action, to symbolise and comment upon it.
—Yasmine Gooneratne, *Jane Austen* (London: Cambridge University Press, 1970), pp. 44–45

❖

## JANE NARDIN ON MANNERS AND MORALITY IN *PRIDE AND PREJUDICE*

[Jane Nardin (b. 1944), a professor of English at the University of Wisconsin, is the author of *Barbara Pym* (1985) and *He Knew She Was Right: The Independent Woman in the Novels of Anthony Trollope* (1989). In this extract from her book on Austen, Nardin explores the relationship between manners and morality in *Pride and Prejudice,* arguing that Austen manages to convince even modern readers of the necessity for strict social standards.]

In *Pride and Prejudice,* Jane Austen makes the basic assumption that a person's outward manners mirror his moral character. If, in this novel, a man or woman always displays good manners, it is perfectly safe for the reader to assume that his character is truly good. The characters in the novel continually try to evaluate one another's manners and the moral worth to which they are a clue. Often these evaluations are wrong, but it is important to note that they are never wrong because the manners of the individual in question have lied about his character. If an attempt to judge character from manners backfires in the world of *Pride and Prejudice,* it is invariably either because the judging individual has misperceived the nature of the manners of the individual he is judging, or because the standard of propriety according to which the judgment is being made is a mistaken one. The problem of judgment in *Pride and Prejudice* is not, as it is in *Persuasion,* for example, primarily a question of penetrating behind the facade of the manners to the reality of moral character; rather it is a question of perceiving and estimating the nature of an individual's manners with a reasonable degree of accuracy.

In a novel where a person's public manners are assumed to be an accurate clue to his private character, the definition of what truly proper manners actually are has an extraordinary importance. The reader must be convinced that the standard of propriety in question is one to which intelligent people of good feeling can give their wholehearted adherence. Jane Austen, it seems to me, achieves this aim in *Pride and Prejudice.* Elizabeth Bennet's standards of decorous behavior do not grate upon the reader's sensibilities as, for example, Elinor Dashwood's excessively rigid and stoical conception of propriety sometimes does. Yet Elizabeth's standards of propriety, at least at the close of the novel, are being presented as identical to the best standards of proper behavior held by her society, as well as identical to the standards of the novel as a whole—and so conformist an ethic might be expected to offend modern readers.

Jane Austen manages to get her readers—even most of her twentieth-century readers—to approve Elizabeth's adherence to a socially acceptable standard of propriety by employing a variety of subtly concealed persuasive techniques. The definition of true propriety which *Pride and Prejudice* offers—to anticipate somewhat—is simply a healthy respect for the conventional rules of social behavior, modified by an understanding that those forms are important, not as ends in themselves, but as means of regulating social intercourse, and that therefore they need not always be followed slavishly.

> —Jane Nardin, *Those Elegant Decorums: The Concept of Propriety in Jane Austen's Novels* (Albany: State University of New York Press, 1973), pp. 47–48

❖

[Lloyd W. Brown (b. 1938), a professor of comparative literature at the University of Southern California, is the author of *Bits of Ivory: Narrative Technique in Jane Austen's Fiction* (1973), *Women Writers in Black Africa* (1981), and *West Indian Poetry* (1984). Here, Brown studies the various marriages in *Pride and Prejudice* and notes to what degree the failure of a marriage points not only to a defective moral character but also to the defects of the institution of marriage.]

In *Pride and Prejudice* the scathing dismissal of the Wickhams offers a striking contrast with the ideal implications of Elizabeth's marriage: 'His affection for her soon sunk into indifference; her's lasted a little longer; and in spite of her youth and her manners, she retained all the claims to reputation which her marriage had given her.' In view of the unsavoury personalities of both Lydia and Wickham this emphasis on their marital failure could easily be limited to the moral implications of their characters were it not for the fact that theirs is simply one more marital failure in the novel. In fact all the marriages that are dealt with in any significant detail (and this would exclude the Gardiners) are inadequate. Charlotte Lucas is no less aware than is the reader of the severe limitations of her marriage. And in the Bennets' marriage Austen offers a chilling analysis of what amounts to a malaise, one which not only ensures the failure of the Bennets' marriage but seems certain of repetition in the next generation of couples, the Collinses and Wickhams, for example:

> Had Elizabeth's opinion been all drawn from her own family, she could not have formed a very pleasing picture of conjugal felicity or domestic comfort. Her father captivated by youth and beauty, and that appearance of good humour, which youth and beauty generally give, had married a woman whose weak understanding and illiberal mind, had very early in their marriage put an end to all real affection for her. Respect, esteem, and confidence, had vanished for ever; and all his views of domestic happiness were overthrown. . . . He was fond of the country and of books; and from these tastes had arisen his prin-

cipal enjoyments. To his wife he was very little otherwise indebted, than as her ignorance and folly had contributed to his amusement. This is not the sort of happiness which a man would in general wish to owe to his wife; but where other pow‑ers of entertainment are wanting, the true philosopher will derive benefit from such as are given.

Even those marriages in which the couples seem reasonably satisfied and compatible are also disturbing because they too imply a questionable continuity. Taken together compatible but deficient couples represent the continuation of their inadequa‑cies within an institutional context (marriage) in much the same way that the conflicts and non-communication of the Bennets represent a pervasive and continuous malaise in human values and relationships. The perfect compatibility of the John Dashwoods, for example, rests in the cold-blooded materialism and in the narrow selfishness which they share equally. But more to the point, that compatibility and the marital continuity which it assures throughout the novel underscore the vigour and persistence of the Dashwoods' value system in their soci‑ety. Elinor's and Marianne's marriages represent ideal excep‑tions. The Dashwoods' union is demonstrably a symbolic extension of the prevailing rule: it is part of a total pattern over which their formidable ally Mrs Ferrars presides to the end. Like the Dashwoods themselves the Dashwood marriage is static and mechanical, and that mechanicality reflects the unyielding hardness of the narrow 'sense' which dominates their world and which is also symbolised by the unions of Robert Ferrars and Lucy Steele, Willoughby and Miss Morton, Sir John and Lady Middleton, and Mr and Mrs Palmer. In identifying these defective unions with prevailing social norms Austen is not simply establishing marriage as a symbol of a social malaise, she is also demonstrating that defective marriages of all kinds (like those of the Bennets or the Dashwoods) continue because their causes are rooted in the continuing defects of their social institutions and environment. By a similar token the Elton mar‑riage in *Emma* is doubly disturbing because Mr Elton's role as vicar (like that of Mr Collins in *Pride and Prejudice*) emphasises that the individual defects may be embodied and perpetuated, however undesignedly, by established institutions—marriage *and* the church in this case—through individuals whose moral and intellectual limitations have defined the actual, as opposed to the ideal, functions of these institutions.

—Lloyd W. Brown, "The Business of Marrying and Mothering," *Jane Austen's Achievement,* ed. Juliet McMaster (New York: Barnes & Noble Books, 1976), 34–36

❖

## CLAUDIA L. JOHNSON ON AUSTEN'S DISCREET SOCIAL CRITICISM

[Claudia L. Johnson is a professor of English at Marquette University and the author of *Equivocal Beings: Politics, Gender and Sentimentality in the 1790s* (1995) and *Jane Austen: Women, Politics and the Novel* (1988), from which the following extract is taken. Here, Johnson sees the conflict between Elizabeth and Lady Catherine as emblematic of Austen's tentative and discreet questioning of the class distinctions of her day.]

Austen's simultaneously bold and delicate handling of the confrontation between Elizabeth and Lady Catherine typifies her entire relationship to the novelistic tradition of social criticism under discussion here. The treatment is decisively progressive because Elizabeth does not consider the interests of the ruling class to be morally binding upon her: "Neither duty, nor honour, nor gratitude," Elizabeth holds, "have any possible claim on me, in the present instance. No principle of either, would be violated by my marriage with Mr. Darcy." Defending her love of laughter from charges of cynicism, Elizabeth proclaims, "I hope I never ridicule what is wise or good," and this promise of principled restraint differentiates Elizabeth's laughter from Lydia's animal glee. But at a time when Hannah More, among others, was writing conduct books for the middle classes and tracts for the lower, enjoining both not to question the wisdom of Providence in placing them in humbler spheres, Elizabeth's disclaimer is not quite as innocuous as it may appear, for the point of contention is exactly what or who *is* "wise or good," and Elizabeth appears not to doubt her own qualifications to decide for herself, and has no trouble censuring a Lady's officious airs or ridiculing a pompous patrician with his failure to behave like a gentleman. As far as Elizabeth is concerned, "extraordinary talents or miraculous virtue" will always command her respect, but the "mere stateliness of money and rank" will not awe her. Convinced that they occupied high ground, progressive novelists seize on the same kinds of distinctions and exploit them for all they are worth, contending, more systematically and more conspicuously of course, that the defenders of money and rank marshal speciously ethical artillery—such as Lady Catherine's "duty," "honour," and "gratitude"—in order to sustain their hegemony, and that it is only by force of "prejudice" that we are either bullied or duped into equating our moral imperatives with their interests.

Although this much is clearly true, the conflict between Elizabeth and Lady Catherine nevertheless remains exceedingly discreet in that even as it demarcates this politically volatile issue, it circumnavigates it at the same time. Austen dramatizes social prejudice, and her revised title highlights that buzzword. But people lower on the social scale can be prejudiced too, and the disputants themselves stand well back from polemical jargon. *Pride and Prejudice* thus alternately verges on and recoils from radical criticism: Lady Catherine is not quite so extreme as to claim outright that the well-being of the kingdom depends on the purity of her family line. And for her part, Elizabeth claims not that she has the right to quit the "sphere" of her birth, but rather that in marrying Darcy, she would be staying within that sphere: "He is a gentleman; I am a gentleman's daughter; so far we are equal." To the extent that this assertion of equality demystifies the great gentry, it serves reformist ends, for it deprives men like Darcy of any rationale for their pride. But in the meantime, it leaves the social structure radicals had assailed substantially intact. Elizabeth, after all, changes her mind about Darcy when she realizes how conscientiously he tends to the happiness of those in his charge as a good master, landlord, and brother: "How many people's happiness were in his guardianship!—How much of pleasure or pain it was in his power to bestow."

The challenge Elizabeth poses to the power of rank and wealth is further diminished when we consider Lady Catherine's sex as well as her utter ridiculousness. Unlike Mrs. Smith in *Sense and Sensibility* and Lady Russell in *Persuasion,* who both figure as alternatives to male authority, women such as Lady Catherine and Mrs. Ferrars are parodies of male authority. As such, although they defend and collude in the interests of the patriarchal family, they themselves obviously are not the most formidable embodiments of it. Because these surrogates are easier to assail than, say, fathers and uncles, they make it possible to show what is oppressive about the power of rank and wealth, and what is overbearing about their assumptions of superiority. Further, they also make it possible to represent rebellion against the claims of familial authority, because in Austen's novels, at least, female authority figures are invariably defied by their young male relations. Though they may hold some purse strings, they hold virtually no moral sway. Because they cannot enforce obedience, their imperiousness is risible. This need not have been so. Austen could have endowed Lady Catherine with some of the daunting majesty Burney extends to Mrs. Delvile in *Cecilia,* for example, a figure who for similar reasons makes similar appeals to the heroine's honor and gratitude, but who does command the respect and voluntary obedience of both her son and Cecilia. But far from being dignified, Lady Catherine is in her own way every bit as ludicrous as Mrs. Bennet. If Austen's use of a weak and ridiculous female authority figure makes it possible to dramatize effectual resistance, it is at the cost of minimizing the extent and perhaps even obscuring the object of that resistance. Quite simply, it is left unclear whether all attempts on the part of the high and mighty to meddle in the autonomous choices of others are to be deemed insufferable, or whether it is merely that Lady Catherine's attempts to wield power are incompetent, inappropriate and eccentric.

—Claudia L. Johnson, Jane Austen: Women, Politics and the Novel (Chicago: University of Chicago Press, 1988), pp. 87–88

❖

[Laura G. Mooneyham is a professor of English at Trinity University in San Antonio, Texas, and the author of *Romance, Language and Education in Jane Austen's Novels* (1988), from which the following extract is taken. Here, Mooneyham argues that the central relationship between Elizabeth and Darcy provides not merely the plot of *Pride and Prejudice* but also its structure.]

The secret of *Pride and Prejudice*'s popularity lies in the dynamics between its hero and heroine. The spark of their relationship depends on their equality of intelligence and perception, for Elizabeth and Darcy are more fully equal in this sense than any other of Austen's protagonists. Each is both protagonist and antagonist; that is, their struggle is as much against each other as it is against the pressures of society or family. The novel presents a balance of power not only between two characters but between two conflicting modes of judgment, and, by extension, between two conflicting systems of language which both reflect and shape these judgments. *Pride and Prejudice* resolves these conflicts in a compromise; Darcy and Elizabeth both change, though in different directions. Furthermore, in *Pride and Prejudice,* the resolution of the romance does not hinge on the capitulation of either lover to the other, as it does in some other Austen novels. For instance, in *Northanger Abbey,* Catherine Morland resolves to think and judge as Henry Tilney does. Edmund comes round to Fanny at the end of *Mansfield Park,* acknowledging his past errors and Fanny's wisdom; the heroine of *Emma* renounces her role as imaginist and binds herself to Mr. Knightley. And in *Persuasion,* Wentworth finds at the novel's conclusion that he owes his happiness less to his own efforts than to Anne's. However, at the end of *Pride and Prejudice,* though both lovers gallantly assume a more than equal share of the blame, the true portion of responsibility for their initial misery and later happiness is in equilibrium. Equality of errors lead to equality of education.

*Pride and Prejudice* is also the only one of Austen's novels which owes its central structure to the relationship between hero and heroine. The actions of the hero in the other five novels are of secondary importance to the design of plot. The architecture of *Northanger Abbey* is determined by the two stages of Catherine's education, by her learning the pitfalls of verbal language at Bath and written language at the Abbey. *Sense and Sensibility*'s structure is determined by the dialectic of Elinor's sense opposed to Marianne's sensibility. *Mansfield Park* is organized around Fanny as an isolated figure among public scenes of general folly—Sotherton, the theatre, the ball, Portsmouth—while the sexual dynamics between herself and Edmund are left almost wholly unexplored. In *Emma,* the structure depends upon the stages of Emma's progress from error to understanding; Mr. Knightley's and Emma's mutual attraction remains a sub-text, ever-present but not the subject of narrative focus until Emma herself acknowledges her feelings midway through Volume III. The relationship between Anne and Wentworth is central to *Persuasion,* but even here structure is determined by Anne's displacement from Kellynch and her changing status from distanced observer to central participant in the action. But in *Pride and Prejudice,* the structure is a product of the relationship between Elizabeth and Darcy. The novel's pace is characterized by a rising intensity when Elizabeth and Darcy are together, and a lull, a sense of intermission, when they are apart. Since the structure results from the dynamics of attraction and antagonism between hero and heroine, it is appropriate that Darcy's first proposal to Elizabeth marks almost the exact centre of the novel. Thus *Pride and Prejudice* in its first half chronicles the growing consequences of those vices in Darcy and Elizabeth which form its title, moves at its centre to the open expression of pride and prejudice in a love scene gone desperately sour, and in its second half traces the resolution of this disunion, the compromises made in the name of love.

—Laura G. Mooneyham, *Romance, Language and Education in Jane Austen's Novels* (New York: St. Martin's Press, 1988), pp. 45–46

❖

[Gene Koppel is a professor of English at the University of Arizona. He is coauthor of *Isaac Bashevis Singer on Literature and Life* (1979) and author of *The Religious Dimensions of Jane Austen's Novels* (1988), from which the following extract is taken. Here, Koppel argues that Austen's religious principles manifest themselves in the "compulsive egotism" of her heroines.]

To serve God and one's fellow man in every significant phase of daily life was ⟨. . .⟩ a major goal of Jane Austen's religion; the immense difficulty of such an ideal clearly makes itself felt both in her prayer and in her fiction. Indeed, the logic, though not the language, of the prayer can be easily traced in the novels: "Teach us to understand the sinfulness of our own hearts, and bring to our knowledge every fault of temper and every evil habit in which we have indulged to the discomfort of our fellow-creatures, and the danger of our own souls," is a religious way of describing the striving for self-knowledge central to the growth of Jane Austen's characters. The compulsive egotism—I suggest that this phrase might serve as a psychological definition of original sin in Austen's fiction—which makes self-recognition and personal growth brutally difficult for any human being is present in the struggles of each of Jane Austen's heroines. Elizabeth Bennet is extremely attractive; her egotism is certainly less spectacular than that of the adolescent Marianne Dashwood or the barely redeemable Emma Woodhouse—but it is there, nonetheless. Only Elizabeth's exuberant charm keeps the reader from responding with shock to the raw arrogance of her reply to Bingley's good-humored admission during their conversation of Netherfield that perhaps, since Elizabeth can see through him so easily, his character is a "pitiful" one: "That is as it happens. It does not necessarily follow that a deep, intricate character is more or less estimable than such a one as yours." Mrs. Bennet is entirely in the right when she immediately reprimands Elizabeth not to "run on in the wild manner that you are suffered to do at home." Along with being a heroine, then, Elizabeth is also daddy's spoiled little darling. It is part of Jane Austen's genius as a writer that Elizabeth's illusion that she, like her father, can easily see through all of the inferior mortals who surround her—an illusion with psychological, moral, and spiritual implications—provides the romantic complications for the plot when Elizabeth pitifully fails to read Darcy's and Wickham's characters during the early stages of their relationships.

Again, it is significant morally as well as romantically that the twin shocks of Darcy's letter and the visit to Pemberley shatter Elizabeth's illusion of omniscience and educate her to her own limitations as well as to Darcy's true value. Since habitual behavior patterns dominate one through the subconscious, only the kind of shock which comes from a serious mistake can provide the opportunity and the motivation for Elizabeth to reevaluate objectively her unquestioned "habitual principles," to use a phrase from a moral writer (Thomas Gisborne) whom Jane Austen favored. Elizabeth must and does prove herself strong enough to recognize the truth when it is thrust upon her. In this she resembles Marianne Dashwood, Emma Woodhouse, and Frederick Wentworth, who learn from their self-induced catastrophes (though the first two of these characters, like Fielding's Tom Jones, need multiple, or even life-threatening, disasters to teach them a lasting lesson).

Darcy goes through a similar though less drastic process: Elizabeth's spirited rejection of his first proposal provides him with the catalyst to reexamine his habitual way of dealing with people, including prospective mates. Thus in the case of both heroine and hero, the major obstacles to their psychological, moral, and spiritual growth and to their worldly happiness are the same, and are cleared away at once; in *Pride and Prejudice,* and in the rest of Austen's fiction, there is essential unity of the dramatic, psychological, moral, and spiritual dimensions.

—Gene Koppel, *The Religious Dimension of Jane Austen's Novels* (Ann Arbor: UMI Research Press, 1988), pp. 8–9

❖

[John A. Dussinger (b. 1935), a professor of English at the University of Illinois, is the author of *The Discourse of Mind in Eighteenth-Century Fiction* (1974) and *In the Pride of the Moment: Encounters in Jane Austen's World* (1989), from which the following extract is taken. Here, Dussinger believes that Mrs. Bennet's speech and silence are used as a means of exercising power in a society dominated by men.]

Talk as oral aggression and silence as defense, a frequent pattern in *Sense and Sensibility,* are keyed in the structure of *Pride and Prejudice,* where the conflict between parents and children becomes a major subject in the narrative. Introduced flatly as a "woman of mean understanding, little information, and uncertain temper," Mrs. Bennet's discourse promises to be tedious and yet unexpectedly throws light on the central agon. Though not so repetitive as Mrs. Allen's preoccupation with clothes, the same refrain of material/moral dichotomy appears in her good opinion of Mrs. Hurst's gown, of Colonel Forster's regimentals, of Mrs. Gardiner's information about long sleeves, and of Lydia's marriage once "all the particulars of calico, muslin, and cambric" are decided. Unlike Mrs. Jennings's matchmaking pursuit, Mrs. Bennet's obsessive interest is in the economic disposal of her children without any sentimental lingering: "If I can but see one of my daughters happily settled at Netherfield . . . and all the others equally well married, I shall have nothing to wish for." An insensitive manipulator, she interferes even to the extent of commanding her daughter to accept a ridiculous marriage proposal: "Lizzy, I *insist* upon your staying and hearing Mr. Collins." Possessing few redeeming qualities, this character functions mainly as an obstacle, a *sena irata* of comedy, whose tactless words threaten the progress of romance.

Though outré in the manner of Mrs. Allen and Mrs. Jennings, Mrs. Bennet's principal role in the novel is to compensate for woman's inferior social position by wielding power through offensive speech and by resorting to her "nerves" as a defense whenever convenient. Often she is a mouthpiece to spew out ideas prohibited in civil conversation but relevant to the circumstances, as is demonstrated emphatically in the scene upon Elizabeth's return from Hunsford:

> "And so, I suppose, they often talk of having Longbourn when your father is dead. They look upon it quite as their own, I dare say, whenever that happens."
> "It was a subject which they could not mention before me."
> "No. It would have been strange if they had. But I make no doubt, they often talk of it between themselves."

To suspect the Collinses of gloating over their eventual inheritance of Longbourn may betray a "mean understanding" and "little information," but granted the egocentric norm of this comic world it is distinctly possible that they *do,* after all, "often talk of it between themselves." Mr. Collins's previous gesture of "atonement" to the Bennets made plain that the entail was very much on his mind, and Mrs. Bennet has good reason to believe that the "Lucases are very artful people indeed."

Despite her muddled reasoning in an argument, Mrs. Bennet is at times disquietingly right about other characters; and her talk has the advantage of filling in many empty spaces in the dialogue and narrative, and of thus imitating the reader's activity. As is already clear from the opening chapter of the novel, her speech has two basic functions: to play alazon to the other's eiron in dialogue, and to demonstrate the false intent of polite conversation. But indirectly, her free talk is useful in expressing the various moods of frustration that arise from woman's subjugation in a male-dominated society; hence, as if to reify a self perpetually disappearing in a void, her words explode spontaneously to release energy and create a presence.

The Bennets' humorous dialogue plays upon the motif of marital asymmetry, the ideal situation for point/counterpoint discourses, which intrigued the author in the lives of her real acquaintances and recurs throughout her novels. Mrs. Allen ⟨in *Northanger Abbey*⟩, for instance, "was one of that numerous class of females, whose society can raise no other emotion than surprise at there being any men in the world who could like them well enough to marry them." The Allen marriage, we have seen, is a schizoidal partnership; and a similar defensive withdrawal afflicts other couples, like the Palmers, the Collinses, the John Knightleys, and the Bertrams. ⟨In *Sense and Sensibility*⟩ Mrs. Palmer's disposition, "strongly endowed by nature with a turn for being uniformly civil and happy," is the elixir that enables two disparate individuals to interact harmoniously, " 'Mr. Palmer is so droll! . . . He is always out of humour.' " The usual rhetorical pattern of these asymmetrical couples sets in opposition a malcontent who refuses either to talk amiably or to talk at all and a gregarious character who talks uncontrollably; and in all of this comic exchange we see the persistent loneliness of selfhood. Although not really a conversation, nevertheless if it proves to be a euphoric experience, talk can be another play activity for escaping self-consciousness.

—John A. Dussinger, *In the Pride of the Moment: Encounters in Jane Austen's World* (Columbus: Ohio State University Press, 1990), pp. 121–23

❖

## JAN FERGUS ON LANGUAGE AND SEXUAL DESIRE IN *PRIDE AND PREJUDICE*

[Jan Fergus (b. 1943) is a professor of English at Lehigh University. She has written *Jane Austen and the Didactic Novel* (1983) and *Jane Austen: A Literary Life* (1991), from which the following extract is taken. Here, Fergus examines how Austen reveals, beneath restrained social discourse, sexual themes in *Pride and Prejudice*.]

One of the great triumphs of *Pride and Prejudice* lies in the way that Austen creates conversations that permit characters to expose, beneath the surface restraints of polite, clever talk, their unstated and incongruous or clashing motives, judgements and feelings. The scenes between Darcy and Elizabeth at Netherfield and Rosings have undercurrents of sexual antagonism and attraction not entirely contained by the comedy of misjudgement enacted on the surface, or by the structural irony which allows Elizabeth's and Darcy's misjudgements of each other to be felt again and again throughout the novel. If substantial revisions or alterations *were* made to *First Impressions* when Austen cut it before publishing it in 1813, they may have been to these scenes, which are unlike any in *Sense and Sensibility* or *Northanger Abbey* as we have them. In their complexity, depth and tension, they more closely resemble the scenes that Austen was writing in 1811–13 for *Mansfield Park.*

The process by which Darcy in these scenes at Netherfield and Rosings interprets Elizabeth's provocative, impertinent manner to him as liveliness, misinterprets it as interest, and finds her attractive, is not simply a matter of 'reading,' an intellectual exercise. It is a sexual response, in keeping with the open way that sexuality is treated in *Pride and Prejudice.* In her treatment of sexuality, Austen the novelist gets away with murder almost as much as Elizabeth does. Admittedly, Austen attributes the most open sexual responses not to her heroine but to Lydia Bennet, who unabashedly enjoys sex before marriage and initiates a spot of cross-dressing as well, when she and her friends dress an officer in one of Mrs Phillips' gowns:

> 'you cannot imagine how well he looked! When Denny, and Wickham, and Pratt, and two or three more of the men came in, they did not know him in the least. Lord! how I laughed! and so did Mrs Forster. I thought I should have died. And *that* made the men suspect something, and then they soon found out what was the matter.'

Lydia, of course, is a foil to Elizabeth, an example of unrestrained sexuality and independence. But by allowing her heroine Elizabeth to exhibit such open sexual response to Wickham's charm, Austen is violating some of the rules that govern many women writers in the period. Delicacy and purity were expected of them; even Austen herself expected it to some degree, as is apparent in her comment on Madame de Genlis' beginning her novel *Alphonsine: or Maternal Affection* (1806) with a detailed account of a wife who, refusing to consummate her marriage, takes a lover and is afterwards surprised by her husband in bed with yet another lover, a servant:

> 'Alphonsine' did not do. We were disgusted in twenty pages, as, independent of a bad translation, it has indelicacies which disgrace a pen hitherto so pure.

Austen's interest lies in portraying not this sort of sensational sexuality, but rather the public sexuality of daily life—attraction, flirtation, infatuation, sexual antagonism and sexual love. As noted earlier, her realistic portraits of women's sexual attraction to men seem unprecedented to a male reviewer writing a few years after her death. Richard Whately praises Austen's willingness to show that women respond to male beauty and charm, but he unfortunately does so at all women's expense: 'Her heroines are what one knows women must be, though one never can get them to admit it'. Whately does not seem to recognise how stringently women during this period were enjoined not to admit their sexual feelings. He is wrong to blame them for what social mores force upon them, but he is right to notice how different Austen's heroines are. Elizabeth in particular is ready to flirt openly with Wickham, attracted by his looks and manner, and she is equally ready to allow an involuntary sexual response to Darcy's powerful presence to feed the hostility awakened by his insulting refusal to dance with her.

—Jan Fergus, *Jane Austen: A Literary Life* (New York: St. Martin's Press, 1991), pp. 84–85

❖

OLIVER MACDONAGH ON THE OVERABUNDANCE OF GIRLS IN *PRIDE AND PREJUDICE*

[Oliver MacDonagh, an historian of Irish culture and a literary critic, is the author of *Ireland* (1968) and *Irish Culture and Nationalism 1750–1950* (1983). In this extract from his book on Austen, MacDonagh comments on the number of eligible girls in *Pride and Prejudice* and their significance to the plot.]

In every sense, girls are the problem in *Pride and Prejudice*. The Bennets' superfluity of daughters and lack of a male heir form the book's central difficulty. The Lucases share the first part of this difficulty, in a lesser form. Miss Darcy has been (and to some extent still is) a problem for her brother. Miss Bingley's problem is to dispose of herself as she desires. The heiresses, great and small, Anne de Bourgh and Mary King, are problems for their mothers to dispose of. At least eight girls in the novel (stretching the term 'girl' to cover at least a twelve-year span in age) are fully, or fairly fully, delineated. Their characters and prospects vary widely. But all pose essentially the same question to themselves or others—how were they to be settled in the world?

The Bennet girls form the book's core group. Each has the identical disadvantage of a negligible dowry (£1,000 at most after their parents' deaths) and the prospect of a calamitous decline in social significance after their middle-aged father dies and the family estate passes into other hands. Elizabeth and Lydia Bennet are the counterparts of Catherine Morland and Isabella Thorpe, standing respectively for what is commendatory and condemnatory in girls. The first pair are much the more finely and intricately drawn as characters, but the respective roles are substantially the same. Elizabeth is three years older than Catherine, far more sophisticated, far cleverer, wittier and (despite her disclaimer that she is '*not* a great reader' and—to Darcy—'Books—Oh! no.—I am sure we never read the same') probably much the better read. Yet she undergoes a similar change to Catherine. Albeit at greater depth at each particular stage, she grows from girlhood to young womanhood during the novel's span.

For all her confidence in her own judgment, Elizabeth was for long too callow to value either Darcy or Wickham at his true worth. Perhaps the usual attribution of qualities should be here reversed. Pride, and its cousin vanity, were *her* particular blinkers in this case, just as the prejudices of class and conventionality were Darcy's. (Characteristically, he observes early in the piece that the Bennet girls' 'low connections' would ' "very materially lessen their chance of marrying men of any consideration in the world" '). Elizabeth was piqued that Darcy, at first meeting, thought her only 'tolerable' in looks and probably a bore to dance with. Then mortification was heaped upon mortification at the Bingleys' ball when one member after another of her family exposed their vulgarity, folly or indecorum to his disdain. Her humiliation fed her enmity towards him for a time.

Conversely, she was flattered, and her judgment accordingly warped, by Wickham's initial attentions. He was, after all, 'the happy man towards whom almost every female eye was turned' when he entered the Philips' drawing-room, 'and Elizabeth was the happy woman by whom he finally seated himself.' Later, she was so infatuated by his continued preference for her as to tell her aunt that

> 'he is, beyond all comparison, the most agreeable man I ever saw—and if he becomes really attached to me—I believe it will be better that he should not. I see the imprudence of it . . . [but] how can I promise to be wiser than so many of my fellow creatures if I am tempted, or how am I even to know that it would be wisdom to resist?'

—Oliver MacDonagh, *Jane Austen: Real and Imagined Worlds* (New Haven: Yale University Press, 1991), 89–90

❖

## Maaja A. Stewart on Dialogue and Authority in *Pride and Prejudice*

[Maaja A. Stewart is a professor of English at Tulane University. In this extract, taken from her book on Austen, Stewart examines an early comic passage featuring Mrs. Bennet, noting that women in the novel can subvert men's power in conversation but not in reality.]

For me, the major characteristic of *Pride and Prejudice* is the wide disparity between the feeling of the foregrounded immediate experience and the dominant judgment of value. This disparity is expressed in extreme form in the opposition of Elizabeth's wit to Darcy's judgment. Elizabeth's generous and entertaining perspective always mediates the immediate scene, which therefore seems rich, full, and free. Hidden behind the immediate scene and becoming visible more quickly to the reader than to Elizabeth are the large patterns of power that render Elizabeth completely helpless. These patterns of power include the patrilineal transmission of property, the social vulnerability of women not protected by men, and the social codes of propriety that deny women the ability to initiate action.

The comic irony in the narrative voice expresses the awareness of female powerlessness long before Elizabeth voices it in the text. The narrrator expresses it, in fact, on the first page of the novel. The urgency of Mrs. Bennet's modal verbs—"you must know . . . must do . . . must feel"—fills the pages of the initial chapter with her words and her desire. Her desire has even appropriated the narrative voice in the opening sentence. In turn, the narrative voice has appropriated the solemn sentence patterns of male moralism: "It is a truth universally acknowledged that . . . ." Mrs. Bennet's desire comically creates a society in which single wealthy men, not dowerless daughters, constitute the glut on the marriage market. The comedy in the first chapter derives from Mrs. Bennet's failure to acknowledge the powerlessness that the scene dramatizes. Although Mrs. Bennet controls the conversation, Mr. Bennet controls the fulfillment of her desire. Only he can do the visiting that would then make the proper introductions and the desired marriage a possibility. The contrast between female desire and male power determines the structure of the novel: no matter how much the women expect or plan, fulfillment depends upon the men. Women's desire, in its own powerlessness and desperation, insistently fictionalizes reality throughout *Pride and Prejudice* as it tries to impose the structure of *must, will, ought,* and *would* on the world controlled by the *is* of man's power.

Elizabeth resists the fictionalizing that characterizes her mother by questioning and mocking the *ought*s of desire, as well as the *must*s of social codes. Her situation in the larger narrative structure, however, is analogous to that of her mother in the first chapter. She also lacks choices, she also cannot initiate action, and she also dominates the immediate scene with speech that controls the subject of conversation but cannot control the reality behind the subject. More important, although she resists the fictions of her mother, she participates in the fictions of her father, becoming wholly complicit with patriarchal evaluations when she falls in love with Darcy. This novel, more than any other by Austen, privileges the assumptions of authority of the father and idealizes the traditional estate.

—Maaja A. Stewart, *Domestic Realities and Imperial Fictions: Jane Austen's Novels in Eighteenth-Century Contexts* (Athens: University of Georgia Press, 1993), pp. 40–41

❖

# Works by
# Jane Austen

*Sense and Sensibility.* 1811. 3 vols.

*Pride and Prejudice.* 1813. 3 vols.

*Mansfield Park.* 1814. 3 vols.

*Emma.* 1816. 3 vols.

*Northanger Abbey and Persuasion.* 1818. 4 vols.

*Novels.* 1833. 5 vols.

*Letters.* Ed. Edward, Lord Brabourne. 1884. 2 vols.

*Novels.* Ed. Reginald Brimley Johnson. 1892. 10 vols.

*Charades &c., Written a Hundred Years Ago by Jane Austen and Her Family.* 1895.

*Love and Freindship.* 1922.

*Novels.* Ed. R. W. Chapman. 1923, 1926, 1933. 5 vols.

*The Watsons.* 1923.

*Five Letters to Her Niece Fanny Knight.* 1924.

*Letters.* Ed. R. Brimley Johnson. 1925.

*Lady Susan.* Ed. R. W. Chapman. 1925.

*Fragment of a Novel Written by Jane Austen, January–March 1817 ⟨Sanditon⟩.* Ed. R. W. Chapman. 1925.

*Plan of a Novel.* Ed. R. W. Chapman. 1926.

*Letters to Her Sister Cassandra and Others.* Ed. R. W. Chapman. 1932.

*Volume the First.* Ed. R. W. Chapman. 1933.

*Three Evening Prayers.* 1940.

*Volume the Third.* Ed. R. W. Chapman. 1951.

*Minor Works.* Ed. R. W. Chapman. 1954.

*Volume the Third.* Ed. Brian Southam. 1963.

*Jane Austen's "Sir Charles Grandison."* Ed. Brian Southam. 1980.

*The Juvenilia of Jane Austen and Charlotte Brontë.* Ed. Frances Beer. 1986.

*Jane Austen's Manuscript Letters in Facsimile.* Ed. Jo Modert. 1990.

*Catharine and Other Writings.* Ed. Margaret Anne Doody and Douglas Murray. 1993.

*The History of England: From the Reign of Henry the 4th to the Death of Charles the 1st.* 1993.

# Works about Jane Austen and Pride and Prejudice

Babb, Howard. *Jane Austen's Novels: The Fabric of Dialogue.* Columbus: Ohio State University Press, 1962.

Berger, Carole. "The Rake and the Reader in Jane Austen's Novels." *Studies in English Literature 1500–1900* 15 (1975): 531–44.

Bloom, Harold, ed. *Jane Austen.* New York: Chelsea House, 1986.

———, ed. *Jane Austen's* Pride and Prejudice. New York: Chelsea House, 1987.

Bradbrook, Frank. *Jane Austen and Her Predecessors.* Cambridge: Cambridge University Press, 1967.

Brown, Julia Prewitt. *Jane Austen's Novels: Social Change and Literary Form.* Cambridge, MA: Harvard University Press, 1979.

Brown, Lloyd W. *Bits of Ivory: Narrative Techniques in Jane Austen's Novels.* Baton Rouge: Louisiana State University Press, 1973.

Bush, Douglas. *Jane Austen.* New York: Macmillan, 1975.

Butler, Marilyn. *Jane Austen and the War of Ideas.* Oxford: Oxford University Press, 1975.

Collins, Irene. *Jane Austen and the Clergy.* London: Hambledon Press, 1993.

DeRose, Peter. "Marriage and Self-Knowledge in *Emma* and *Pride and Prejudice.*" *Renascence* 30 (1978): 199–216.

Devlin, David. *Jane Austen and Education.* New York: Barnes & Noble, 1973.

Duckworth, Alistair. *The Improvement of the Estate: A Study of Jane Austen's Novels.* Baltimore: Johns Hopkins University Press, 1971.

Ehrenpreis, Irvin. "Austen: The Heroism of the Quotidian." In Ehrenpreis's *Acts of Implication: Suggestion and Covert Meaning in the Works of Dryden, Swift, Pope, and Austen.* Berkeley: University of California Press, 1980, pp. 112–45.

Fergus, Jan. *Jane Austen and the Didactic Novel.* Totowa, NJ: Barnes & Noble, 1983.

Gard, Roger. *Jane Austen's Novels: The Art of Clarity.* New Haven: Yale University Press, 1992.

Grey, J. David, ed. *The Jane Austen Companion.* New York: Macmillan, 1986.

Halperin, John. *The Life of Jane Austen.* Baltimore: Johns Hopkins University Press, 1984.

Hardy, Barbara. *A Reading of Jane Austen.* New York: New York University Press, 1976.

Hardy, John. *Jane Austen's Heroines: Intimacy in Human Relationships.* London: Routledge & Kegan Paul, 1984.

Harris, Jocelyn. *Jane Austen's Art of Memory.* Cambridge: Cambridge University Press, 1989.

Honan, Park. *Jane Austen: Her Life.* New York: St. Martin's Press, 1987.

Kaplan, Deborah. *Jane Austen among Women.* Baltimore: Johns Hopkins University Press, 1992.

Kelly, G. "The Art of Reading in *Pride and Prejudice.*" *English Studies in Canada* 10 (1984): 156–71.

Kroeber, Karl. *Styles in Fictional Structure: The Art of Jane Austen, Charlotte Brontë, George Eliot.* Princeton: Princeton University Press, 1971.

Lauber, John. *Jane Austen.* New York: Twayne, 1993.

Litz, A. Walton. *Jane Austen: A Study of Her Artistic Development.* New York: Oxford University Press, 1965.

McKeon, Richard. "*Pride and Prejudice:* Thought, Character, Argument, and Plot." *Critical Inquiry* 5 (1979): 511–27.

McMaster, Juliet. *Jane Austen on Love.* Victoria, BC: University of Victoria, 1978.

Mansell, Darrel. *The Novels of Jane Austen: An Interpretation.* London: Macmillan, 1973.

Moler, Kenneth L. *Jane Austen's Art of Illusion.* Lincoln: University of Nebraska Press, 1968.

————. Pride and Prejudice: *A Study in Artistic Economy.* Boston: Twayne, 1989.

Monaghan, David. *Jane Austen: Structure and Social Vision.* London: Macmillan, 1980.

Morgan, Susan. *In the Meantime: Character and Perception in Jane Austen's Fiction.* Chicago: University of Chicago Press, 1980.

Mukherjee, Meenakshi. *Jane Austen.* New York: St. Martin's Press, 1991.

Odmark, John. *An Understanding of Jane Austen's Novels.* Oxford: Basil Blackwell, 1972.

Page, Norman. *The Language of Jane Austen.* Oxford: Basil Blackwell, 1972.

Paris, Bernard. *Character and Conflict in Jane Austen's Novels.* Detroit: Wayne State University Press, 1979.

*Persuasions: Journal of the Jane Austen Society of North America.* 1979– .

Phillips, K. C. *Jane Austen's English.* London: Andre Deutsch, 1970.

Polhemus, Robert. *Comic Faith: The Great Tradition from Austen to Joyce.* Chicago: University of Chicago Press, 1980.

Rees, Jane. *Jane Austen: Woman and Writer.* New York: St. Martin's Press, 1976.

Roberts, Warren. *Jane Austen and the French Revolution.* New York: St. Martin's Press, 1979.

Scott, P. J. M. *Jane Austen: A Reassessment.* Totowa, NJ: Barnes & Noble, 1982.

Sherry, James. "*Pride and Prejudice:* The Limits of Society." *Studies in English Literature 1500–1900* 19 (1979): 609–22.

Smith, LeRoy. *Jane Austen and the Drama of Woman.* London: Macmillan, 1983.

Sulloway, Alison G. *Jane Austen and the Province of Womanhood.* Philadelphia: University of Pennsylvania Press, 1989.

Tanner, Tony. *Jane Austen.* Cambridge, MA: Harvard University Press, 1986.

Tave, Stuart M. *Some Words of Jane Austen.* Chicago: University of Chicago Press, 1973.

Thompson, James. *Between Self and World: The Novels of Jane Austen.* University Park: Pennsylvania State University Press, 1988.

Todd, Janet, ed. *Jane Austen: New Perspectives.* New York: Holmes & Meier, 1983.

Tucker, George Holbert. *Jane Austen, the Woman: Some Biographical Insights.* New York: St. Martin's Press, 1994.

Wallace, Robert K. *Jane Austen and Mozart: Classical Equilibrium in Fiction and Music.* Athens: University of Georgia Press, 1983.

Watkins, Susan. *Jane Austen's Town and Country Style.* New York: Rizzoli, 1990.

Weinsheimer, Joel, ed. *Jane Austen Today.* Athens: University of Georgia Press, 1975.

Welty, Eudora. "A Note on Jane Austen." *Shenandoah* 20, No. 3 (Spring 1969): 3–17.

Willis, Lesley H. "Eyes and the Imagery of Sight in *Pride and Prejudice.*" *English Studies in Canada* 2 (1976): 156–62.

Wilt, Judith. "Jane Austen: The Anxieties of Common Life." In Wilt's *Ghosts of the Gothic: Austen, Eliot and Lawrence.* Princeton: Princeton University Press, 1980, pp. 121–72.

Wiltshire, John. *Jane Austen and the Body: "The Picture of Health."* Cambridge: Cambridge University Press, 1992.

# Index of
# Themes and Ideas